DISCARD

Yale Studies in Political Science, 13

David Horne, Editor

Published under the direction of the Department of Political Science

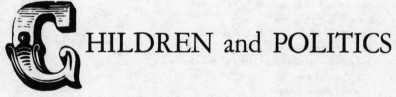

CHILDREN and POLITICS

REVISED EDITION

by Fred I. Greenstein

New Haven and London, Yale University Press

*Originally published with assistance from the
foundation established in memory of
Philip Hamilton McMillan
of the Class of 1894, Yale College.*

*Copyright © 1965 by Yale University.
Revised edition © 1969 by Yale University.
Seventh printing, 1974.
Designed by John O. C. McCrillis,
set in Linotype Garamond,
and printed in the United States of America by
The Colonial Press Inc.,
Clinton, Massachusetts.
Library of Congress catalog card number: 65–11181
ISBN: 0–300–01319–1 (cloth), 0–300–01320–5 (paper)*

*Published in Great Britain, Europe, and Africa by
Yale University Press, Ltd., London.
Distributed in Latin America by Kaiman & Polon, Inc., New York City;
in Australasia and Southeast Asia by John Wiley & Sons
Australasia Pty. Ltd., Sydney;
in India by UBS Publishers' Distributors Pvt., Ltd., Delhi;
in Japan by John Weatherhill, Inc., Tokyo.*

To my parents

Acknowledgments

From the time in 1956 when it first occurred to me that children's political development might fruitfully be studied, to the present, I have acquired a formidable number of debts. In particular, I want to thank Robert E. Lane, who as dissertation advisor, friend, and colleague, contributed to this work in more ways than can be reckoned. Three other friends, James D. Barber, Elton F. Jackson, and Nelson W. Polsby provided valuable critiques of the final draft of the manuscript.

In addition, at one time or another, I had the benefit of comments and advice from Robert Abelson, Theodore Anderson, Arthur J. Brodbeck, Herbert Jacob, William Kessen, Harold D. Lasswell, Stanley Lebergott, Roger Masters, Frank Pinner, Vladimir Stoikov, Aaron Wildavsky, and Barbara and Raymond Wolfinger.

Thanks also go to Helen Rakieten, elementary education supervisor in the New Haven school system, the 700-odd school children who participated in the various phases of the study (all of whose identities are concealed in the chapters which follow), and Ruth Davis of Yale University Press. The editors and publishers of *The American Political Science Review, The Journal of Politics,* and *Social Forces* have permitted me to reprint and revise material which originally appeared in their journals. Financial support has come from a Yale University Political Science Department Falk Fellowship and from Wesleyan University faculty research funds. The finishing touches were applied to the manuscript while I was a fellow at the Center for Advanced Study in the Behavioral Sciences in the Fall of 1964. I had the good fortune, at that point, to receive a variety of thoughtful suggestions about style and substance from Miriam Gallaher, who proved to be a sensitive and meticulous critic.

The academic wife is customarily thanked for uncomplaining support of her husband's endeavor. It is a pleasure to thank my wife, Barbara, for her assistance—complaints and all—in tasks which ranged from I.B.M. card sorting, through intelligent editorial criticism, to the nonpolitical socialization of our three children in the frequent absence of their father.

F. I. G.

Contents

A man has come into the world; his early years are spent without notice in the pleasures and activities of childhood. As he grows up, the world receives him when his manhood begins, and he enters into contact with his fellows. He is then studied for the first time, and it is imagined that the germ of the vices and the virtues of his maturer years is then formed.

This, if I am not mistaken, is a great error. We must begin higher up; we must watch the infant in his mother's arms; we must see the first images which the external world casts upon the dark mirror of his mind, the first occurrences that he witnesses; we must hear the first words which awaken the sleeping powers of thought, and stand by his earliest efforts if we would understand the prejudices, the habits, and the passions which will rule his life. The entire man is, so to speak, to be seen in the cradle of the child.

Alexis de Tocqueville,
DEMOCRACY IN AMERICA, VOL. I,
Chapter 2

CHAPTER 1

The Study of Early Political Learning

My main concern in this book will be with the political development of children between the ages of nine and thirteen, in the last five years of elementary school. What is the nature of political awareness and involvement during these years? What do children learn about politics? Is the sequence of political learning in childhood significant? Of what relevance is political development during this period for the individual's later political participation and, more generally, for the political system?

The years between nine and thirteen are an undramatic but crucial period of both social–psychological and political development. These, in psychoanalytic parlance, are "latency" years. Although growth continues, there is little during the latency period which compares with the rapid changes, both physiological and psychological, at puberty, or during the first few years of life.

Nevertheless, during the last five years of elementary school, children move from near—but not complete—ignorance of adult politics to awareness of most of the conspicuous features of the adult political arena. And the fourth and eighth graders live in quite different psychosocial worlds.

The nine-year-old is a small child, quite dependent upon parents and other adults. His world is one of toys, games, and fantasy. When we ask fourth graders "What do you like to do when there is no school?" many of them simply say "I like to play." When we ask them what they would like if they could have anything they want, they speak of "a trip to outer space . . . a horse

with a new saddle . . . not to have to eat vegetables . . . a big set
of electric trains . . . a real live pony." By thirteen we find incipient adults; pubertal physiological changes have begun for
most girls and many boys, as has heterosexual interest; the world
now extends far beyond the family and the neighborhood. Eighth
graders like to "get together with friends," "talk on the phone,"
"play records and dance." They wish: "that I will become successful as an aeronautical engineer . . . that we could get a house of
our own . . . to be sixteen and have my own convertible . . . that
I had a boyfriend."

CITIZENSHIP TRAINING: A CLASSICAL CONCERN

Education, interpreting the term in its broadest sense, is a highly efficient (and, in fact, necessary) instrument of politics. Political
behavior, like other forms of behavior, is partially determined by
the "objective" circumstances which surround men—for example,
the political institutions of their society. But behavior also is the
result of learned predispositions—the goals, preferences, conceptions of reality, and loyalties which citizens and their leaders acquire through prior experiences. To the degree that learning has
taken place, it becomes less necessary and often less possible to
influence behavior by external rewards and punishments. Thus,
for example, political authority is likely to be more stable when
it is obeyed automatically because citizens have learned to accept
certain institutions and leaders as legitimate than when sanctions
have to be threatened or employed. And sanctions themselves depend upon learning for their effectiveness. A sanction will work
only if people acquire the motivation to respond to it. Since behavior is in so large a part the consequence of learned predispositions, the study of political learning provides a key vantage from
which to analyze political systems.

No topic of political science has a longer and more distinguished
lineage than citizenship training. For Plato, education was at the
heart of politics; depending upon the nature of civic training, a
body politic would remain stable or it would undergo change. The

concentration on education in Plato's ideal Republic was sufficiently great to lead Rousseau to remark: *"The Republic* is not a
work of politics, as those who only judge books by their titles
think; it is the finest treatise on education that was ever written."[1]
Plato's well-known account of the cycle of degeneration of a body
politic—from aristocracy, through timocracy, oligarchy, and
democracy, to tyranny—is an ingenious analysis of the consequences of defective political education. In this account political
change is marked by the successive rebellion of generations of sons
from the values of their fathers.[2] Aristotle, although perhaps less
"psychological" than his predecessor, took it for granted that "the
legislator should make the education of the young his chief and
foremost concern." Aristotle's interest in "the type of character
appropriate to a constitution" bridges the centuries to contemporary discussions of the psychological requirements of "nation-
building."[3]

Traditional political thought abounds in discussions of the
family and of the authority relations between father and mother,
between parents and children, another indication of the long-
standing interest of students of politics in the antecedents of
citizenship. To varying degrees family experience has been described as the precursor, prototype, and bulwark of political relationships in the larger society. Thus Bodin commented that
"children who stand in little awe of their parents, and have even
less fear of the wrath of God, readily set at defiance the authority
of the magistrates."[4] Hobbes and Locke discussed at length the
structure of authority within families, in each case with explicit
reference to the significance of power within the family for politics
in civil society.[5]

1. J. J. Rousseau, *Émile,* ed. François Pierre Richard (Paris, Garnier, 1957),
p. 10.

2. *The Republic,* viii and ix.

3. *Politics,* vii.1.1.

4. Jean Bodin, *Six Books of the Commonwealth,* trans. M. J. Tooley (New
York, Macmillan, 1955), p. 13.

5. John Locke, *Two Treatises of Government* (New York, Hafner, 1947),
pp. 10–60; Thomas Hobbes, *Leviathan* (Oxford, Blackwell, 1955), pp. 130–32.

In both political folklore ("the hand that rocks the cradle . . .")
and political practice there is substantial preoccupation with training of the young. Leaders are especially likely to see the need of
extensive programs of political education when they perceive elements of potential instability in their system: for instance, when
they are attempting to weld together diverse and antagonistic
populations into a single nation. Napoleon commented in 1808
that, "as long as children are not taught whether they ought to be
Republican or Monarchist, Catholic or irreligious, the State will
not form a Nation."[6] Extensive formal political education also
occurs where, as is the case under totalitarianism, the state attempts
to carry on many of the functions ordinarily performed by other
institutions such as the family. In official Soviet writings, pro-
nouncements such as the following are common: "Today we
should pay special attention to rearing the rising generation in
the spirit of Soviet patriotism and devotion to the cause of communism. . . . The success of upbringing is decided precisely in the
early years, when the character of a person, his attitude toward
people and to life, is being formed."[7]

Yet procedures for civic initiation are equally important, if not
quite as conspicuous, in the Western democracies. In the United
States, children are exposed from an early age to patriotic rituals.
A 1948 survey of *Education for Freedom as Provided by State
Laws* found that all but four of the states had legislative requirements for "instruction on the Constitution" at the elementary
school level.[8] The purposes of such civic instruction are suggested
by the following passage from a 1945 New Jersey statute describing a public school history course.

6. David Thomson, *Democracy in France* (3d ed. London, Oxford University Press, 1958), p. 143.

7. From *Komsomolskaya Pravda*, July 10, 1963, trans. in *The Current
Digest of the Soviet Press, 15* (August 14, 1963), 3–9.

8. Ward W. Keesecker, *Education for Freedom as Provided by State Laws*
(Washington, D.C., Federal Security Agency Bulletin No. 11, 1948), p. 8.
Also see Bessie Louise Pierce, *Citizens' Organizations and the Civic Training
of Youth* (New York, Scribner's, 1933), and *Citizenship Education: A Survey
of Requirements for Citizenship Education Among the 50 States* (New York,
Robert A. Taft Institute of Government, 1963).

Such course of study shall include instruction in the principles and ideals of the American form of representative government as expressed by the framers of the Declaration of Independence and of the Constitution of the United States, in said documents and particularly in the Bill of Rights, and the history of the origin and growth of the social, economic and cultural development of the United States, of American family life, and of the high standard of living and other privileges enjoyed by the citizens of the United States as will tend to instill into every boy and girl a determination to preserve these principles and ideals as the principles and ideals of citizens of the United States, and appreciation of their solemn duty and obligation to exercise the privilege of the ballot, upon their reaching voting age, to the end that such principles and ideals may be preserved.[9]

Much of American civic education takes place informally. From an early age, children learn about government and politics and begin to prepare for their adult political roles, through processes which neither they nor those who instruct them are especially conscious of, but which nevertheless provide the basis of democratic political participation. Political awareness and involvement gradually grow as children are exposed to political events and actors, some of which they experience directly, but more of which they become familiar with through the conversations of adults and peers, and through the mass media.

THE STUDY OF "POLITICAL SOCIALIZATION"

Only since the 1950s has a generic label—"political socialization"—become attached to the process of initiation into politics and have scholars started with some frequency to bemoan that "we know next to nothing about 'political socialization.'"[10] The

---

9. Cited in *Citizenship Education,* pp. 7–8.

10. Heinz Eulau et al., "The Political Socialization of American State Legislators," *Midwest Journal of Political Science,* 3 (1959), 188.

recency of systematic attention to political socialization can be traced to the slow process by which political science established itself as an academic discipline and liberated itself from its origins in departments of law, philosophy, and history, and to disciplinary compartmentalizations which assigned the study of children to psychologists and sociologists. Once defined as a legitimate area of analysis, however, political socialization quickly became the subject of widespread speculation and, to a somewhat lesser degree, research.

As early as the 1920s there were ripples of interest on the part of social scientists in the genesis of individual political behavior. In the late 1920s and early 1930s, the formal aspects of civic training were examined in a collection of studies sponsored by the American Historical Association.[11] During the same years, political development was the subject of a nine-volume series under the editorship of Charles E. Merriam.[12] This cross-cultural collection had the virtue of conceiving political learning comprehensively, as a process not only of childhood training but also of constant reinforcement and learning throughout life. Attention was devoted to the broad range of societal institutions, including parties, private associations, and bureaucracy. The studies were, however, necessarily impressionistic and involved no direct observation of developmental processes. Consideration of pre-adult political development was largely confined to formal analysis of the school system and youth groups. In fact, Merriam, in his summary remarks on agents of political training, did not even refer to the family.[13]

Merriam was well aware of the desirability of direct study of individual political participants, including children. In 1925 he predicted that "the examination of the rise and development of the

11. Representative volumes are Pierce, *Citizens' Organizations and the Civic Training of Youth;* Charles E. Merriam, *Civic Education in the United States* (New York, Scribner's, 1934); Truman L. Kelley and A. C. Krey, *Tests and Measurements in the Social Sciences* (New York, Scribner's, 1934).

12. The summary volume of this series is Charles E. Merriam's *The Making of Citizens* (Chicago, University of Chicago Press, 1931).

13. Ibid., pp. 250–362.

political ideation and the political behavior of the child has in store for us much of value in the scientific understanding of the adult ideal and conduct."[14] Merriam's student, Harold D. Lasswell, guided by his psychoanalytic training, also periodically urged the study of political socialization at all age levels.[15] In 1954, nevertheless, it was still possible for a review of the voting literature to point to the virtual absence of data on children's political development.[16]

By that date a considerable body of research findings had accumulated, partially illuminating the developmental processes leading to adult citizenship. The difficulty was that this research was scattered and it had not been explicitly designed to shed light on the political process. Since no scholars had directed themselves frontally to political socialization, data were not available on the development of many commonplace political orientations—for example, party loyalty. Almost every conceivable politically *related* aspect of social behavior had received some attention. Children's interests and wishes, their fears, the types of people with whom they identify, and their media behavior all had been studied.[17] Educational research in the social studies had touched

14. Charles E. Merriam, *New Aspects of Politics* (Chicago, University of Chicago Press, 1925), p. 85.

15. Harold D. Lasswell, *Psychopathology and Politics,* reprinted in *The Political Writings of Harold D. Lasswell* (Glencoe, The Free Press, 1951), pp. 8 and 61; *Democratic Character,* in ibid.; *Power and Personality* (New York, Norton, 1948), pp. 156–57; "The Selective Effect of Personality on Political Participation," in *Studies in the Scope and Method of "The Authoritarian Personality,"* ed. Richard Christie and Marie Jahoda (Glencoe, The Free Press, 1954), pp. 197–225.

16. Seymour M. Lipset et al., "The Psychology of Voting," in *The Handbook of Social Psychology,* ed. Gardner Lindzey (2 vols. Cambridge, Addison-Wesley, 1954), 2, 1144–45.

17. See, for example, Harold E. Jones, "The Environment and Mental Development," in *Manual of Child Psychology,* ed. Leonard Carmichael (2d ed. New York, Wiley, 1954), pp. 631–96; Arthur T. Jersild and Ruth J. Tasch, *Children's Interests and What They Suggest for Education* (New York, Teacher's College Bureau of Publications, 1959); F. Canonge, "Intérêts et curiosités des élèves de centres d'apprentissage," *Enfance, 1* (1948), 304–15; Arthur T. Jersild, et al., *Children's Fears, Dreams, Wishes, Likes, Dislikes, Pleasant and*

upon political phenomena, but much more in terms of the accuracy of children's textbook learning than in terms of their perceptions of politics and their partisan motivations.[18] Class and ethnic awareness had been shown to be present early in childhood.[19] On the adolescent and post-adolescent level, there had been some specifically political attitude research.[20] The growing literature on adult electoral behavior had begun to include reports of adults' retrospections about their political socialization.[21] And, the thesis that the individual's early experiences affect his later political behavior had received wide currency in a variety of controversial bodies of literature on personality and politics, including

Unpleasant Memories, Child Development Monograph, 12 (1933); David S. Hill, "Personification of Ideals by Urban Children," *Journal of Social Psychology, 1* (1930), 379–92; Frederick J. Meine, "Radio and the Press among Young People," in *Radio Research—1941,* ed. Paul F. Lazarsfeld and Frank Stanton (New York, Duell, Sloan and Pearce, 1942), pp. 189–224; Alice P. Sterner, *Radio, Motion Picture and Reading Interests* (New York, Teacher's College Bureau of Publications, Contributions to Education No. 932, 1947).

18. William H. Burton, *Children's Civic Information* (Los Angeles, University of Southern California Press, 1936); Hyman Meltzer, *Children's Social Concepts: A Study of Their Nature and Development* (New York, Teacher's College Bureau of Publications, Contributions to Education No. 192, 1925); Harry Ordan, *Social Concepts and the Child Mind* (New York, King's Crown Press, 1925); Kelley and Krey, *Tests and Measurements in the Social Sciences.*

19. Bernice L. Neugarten, "Social Class and Friendship among School Children," *American Journal of Sociology, 51* (1946), 305–13; Kenneth B. Clark and Mamie P. Clark, "Racial Identification and Preference in Negro Children," in *Readings in Social Psychology,* ed. Theodore Newcomb and Eugene Hartley (New York, Henry Holt, 1947), pp. 169–78; Mary Ellen Goodman, *Race Awareness in Young Children* (Cambridge, Addison-Wesley, 1952).

20. The studies of the Purdue Opinion Poll's national sample of high school students provide much political survey data. Some of this group's findings are interpreted by Hyman (see n. 23 below). A summary of their work is found in H. H. Remmers and D. H. Radler, *The American Teenager* (New York, Bobbs-Merrill, 1957); Richard Centers, "Children of the New Deal: Social Stratification and Adolescent Attitudes," *International Journal of Opinion and Attitude Research, 4* (1950), 315–17 and 322–35; H. H. Remmers, "Early Socialization of Attitudes," in *American Voting Behavior,* ed. Eugene Burdick and Arthur J. Brodbeck (Glencoe, The Free Press, 1959).

21. For example, Angus Campbell, et al., *The Voter Decides* (Evanston, Row, Peterson, 1954), pp. 97–107.

national character studies, authoritarianism research, and psycho-analytic case studies.[22] In 1959 Herbert Hyman performed the valuable service of assembling certain of the earlier studies and reanalyzing them in terms of their political implications.[23]

In the late 1950s a number of investigators began, largely independently of each other, to launch political socialization research. Early and closely related results of two studies, the present one and the work of Easton and Hess in Chicago, were reported almost simultaneously in 1960.[24] At about the same time a number of interesting theoretical and conceptual discussions of political socialization as a field of inquiry appeared.

HOW TO STUDY POLITICAL SOCIALIZATION

Once the merit of studying political behavior from a developmental standpoint is acknowledged, it becomes evident that a bewilderingly extensive universe for research exists. The antecedents of both mass and elite political behavior can be studied. Political learning takes place not only during the early years with which we are concerned here, but also throughout life, particularly as individuals assume political roles, such as ward chairman, Congressman, bureaucrat. Included in the behavior which may be

22. Clyde Kluckhohn, "Culture and Behavior," in Lindzey, *Handbook of Social Psychology, 2,* 949–52; Alex Inkeles and Daniel J. Levinson, "National Character: The Study of Modal Personality and Sociocultural Systems," ibid., pp. 977–1020; Otto Klineberg, *Tensions Affecting International Understanding* (New York, Social Science Research Council, 1950); Talcott Parsons, "Certain Primary Sources and Patterns of Aggression in the Social Structure of the Western World," *Essays in Sociological Theory Pure and Applied* (Glencoe, The Free Press, 1949); T. W. Adorno, et al., *The Authoritarian Personality* (New York, Harper, 1950); Christie and Jahoda; Richard Christie and Peggy Cook, "A Guide to Published Literature Relating to the Authoritarian Personality through 1956," *Journal of Psychology, 45* (1958), 171–99.

23. Herbert Hyman, *Political Socialization: A Study in the Psychology of Political Behavior* (Glencoe, The Free Press, 1959).

24. Fred I. Greenstein, "The Benevolent Leader: Children's Images of Political Authority," *American Political Science Review, 54* (1960), 934–43; Robert D. Hess and David Easton, "The Child's Image of the President," *The Public Opinion Quarterly, 24* (1960), 632–44.

studied are a wide variety of psychic dispositions—cognitions, attitudes, identifications—and the complex relations between psychic dispositions and action.

If political socialization extends, as it were, vertically into adult political learning, it also extends horizontally into ostensibly nonpolitical learning. Numerous nonpolitical aspects of the ways in which the culture is internalized and personality is formed impinge upon politics and therefore must be investigated. Attention must be devoted to both the socialized and the agents of socialization, with the assumption that the political socialization process varies within and between societies and over time. And, a broad conception of "socialization" involves consideration of how nonconformity as well as conformity is learned—of both discontinuities and continuities in political learning.

Given this formidable complexity, it is not surprising that a number of commentators have felt that systematic conceptual clarification and theorizing are prerequisites to satisfactory political socialization research. Several conceptualizations have been offered. They present an initial impression of a Babel of inconsistency, but on closer examination it is evident that all of them cover portions of the same landscape. They use different terminology to make common, or at least not mutually inconsistent, distinctions.

The leading general formulations are those of Easton and Hess, Froman, Mitchell, Almond, and Pye. Easton and Hess[25] elucidate nine aspects of the content of political learning. They discuss three kinds of acquired orientations—cognitive knowledge, attitudes, and standards of evaluation—as these apply to three aspects of political systems—the incumbent political leadership, the "regime" or form of government, and the political community itself. They then raise questions about the nature of learning within the nine

25. David Easton and Robert D. Hess, "Youth and the Political System," in *Culture and Social Character,* ed. Seymour M. Lipset and Leo Lowenthal (New York, The Free Press of Glencoe, 1961), pp. 226–51; David Easton and Robert D. Hess, "The Child's Political World," *Midwest Journal of Political Science,* 6 (1962), 229–46.

subdivisions—about, for example, the age at which learning takes place and the sequence of learning. Froman[26] is especially concerned with accounting for the learning of political behavior by characterizing an individual's environment (the agents of socialization), his personality (the consequences of socialization), and the feedback of his learned political responses on his personality and environment. Mitchell,[27] like Froman, deals in detail with agents of socialization, and like Easton and Hess offers a classification of what is learned (political motivation, political values, political norms, and political information).

The statements of Almond and Pye on political socialization are closely related to each other. Both were derived from the efforts of the Committee on Comparative Political Behavior of the Social Science Research Council to produce a set of uniform "functional" categories for the analysis of Western and non-Western politics. Almond[28] speaks of "latent" (or "analogous") and "manifest" political socialization. The former is nominally nonpolitical learning (for example, personality development and the acquisition of general cultural values in the family) which in some way affects political behavior; the latter is "explicit transmission of information, values, or feelings vis-à-vis the roles, inputs, and outputs of the political system." He characterizes the learning process in terms of Talcott Parsons' "pattern variables" of diffuseness-specificity, particularism-universalism, affectivity-instrumentality.

Pye[29] refers to the "basic socialization process through which the child is inducted into his particular culture and trained to

26. Lewis A. Froman, Jr., "Personality and Political Socialization," *Journal of Politics, 23* (1961), 341–52.

27. William C. Mitchell, *The American Polity* (New York, The Free Press of Glencoe, 1962), pp. 145–78.

28. Gabriel A. Almond, "A Functional Approach to Comparative Politics," in *The Politics of the Developing Areas,* ed. Gabriel A. Almond and James S. Coleman (Princeton, Princeton University Press, 1960), pp. 26–33.

29. Lucian W. Pye, *Politics, Personality, and Nation Building* (New Haven, Yale University Press, 1962), pp. 44–56, and his "Political Modernization and Research on the Process of Political Socialization," *Items, 13* (1959), 25–28.

become a member of his society," a process which he suggests is followed chronologically by "political socialization through which the individual develops his awareness of his political world and gains his appreciation, judgment, and understanding of political events." Pye conceives of both socialization processes as proceeding at "manifest" and "latent" levels. Manifest basic socialization involves the learning of the content of the individual's culture; latent basic socialization consists of "all the experiences that shape the unconscious and determine the dynamics of the basic personality structure." Political socialization, he argues, is mainly manifest; i.e. it is "governed . . . by perception and cognition and conscious learning." Both Almond and Pye distinguish between socialization processes and recruitment into (active) political roles.

One convenient, if rough, way of combining the basic elements of these various formulations is the following paraphrase of Lasswell's statement of the general process of communication: (1) Who (2) learns what (3) from whom (4) under what circumstances (5) with what effects? Evidently a full-blown characterization of political socialization would include classifications of:

1. *Who learns.* Learning differs according to the social and psychological characteristics of the individuals socialized. These characteristics affect both the educational influences an individual will receive and his receptivity to them. In the study reported here we shall consider the differences in the political learning of boys and girls and of children of upper and lower socioeconomic status. We shall take note of the significance not only of what communications children are exposed to, but also of what they are able to absorb and what they selectively perceive and misperceive.

2. *What is learned.* A broad distinction can be made between specifically political learning and politically related learning, the latter including such aspects of the culture as prevailing views of classes and ethnic groups and such personality predispositions as aggressiveness, orientations toward authority figures, and perceptions of the benignness or malignancy of others in society.

The ways of classifying the specifically political content which is learned are countless and, of course, the usefulness of any classification depends upon the investigative purposes to which it will be turned. One possible classification would distinguish between learning connected with the citizen role (partisan attachment, ideology, motivation to participate), learning connected with the subject role (national loyalty, conceptions of the legitimacy of roles and institutions), and learning connected with the recruitment to and performance of specialized political roles. As we have seen, Easton and Hess offer a classification of the objects about which individuals learn: incumbent leaders, the regime, and the community. At the very least one might want to add objects outside the individual's society, such as other nations. Ordinarily one would want to note not only the objects themselves, but also the dispositions acquired toward these objects. Is the learning mainly cognitive? Is it affective? Normally there is some blend of the two. An especially important class of learning is the development of identifications of the self with others in the immediate and remote environments.

3. *The agents of political socialization.* Among the most obvious sources of political learning in the United States are parents, teachers, neighbors, members of the extended family, peers, and the media of communication and those whose views are transmitted through the media. Part of what is suggested by the distinction Almond and Pye make between manifest and latent socialization is the *intention* of the agent of socialization. Is the socialization conscious and intentional, or is it not?

4. *The circumstances of political socialization.* All of the principles governing the effectiveness of educational practices and, more generally, of communication and persuasion apply to assessing the significance of the various circumstances under which political learning occurs. One aspect of this is the *level of awareness* at which learning takes place. This is a further element in the distinction between manifest and latent political socialization.[30]

30. The terms "manifest" and "latent" are ambiguous, as used by Almond and Pye, because they refer to two phenomena which can vary independently of each other: (1) the degree to which teaching is conscious and intentional,

Sometimes the child's attention is quite consciously and explicitly focused on his political learning. More often, at least in the United States, early political learning has a preconscious quality—the child absorbs political information and attitudes without being particularly aware that he is doing so, although what he has absorbed is readily capable of being brought to consciousness. (And, as we shall see, it is probably significant that a number of political orientations are acquired in this inadvertent fashion.) Finally, some political and politically related learning seems to be unconscious in the sense of being repressed and inaccessible to waking awareness.[31]

Another circumstance of learning is the *sequence* in which political orientations are acquired. Here, it is important to consider not only the order of learning, but also whether the learning takes place quite early in life, before critical capacities are formed, or at a later, more skeptical stage.[32]

5. *The effects of political learning.* One important task for research is to establish the effects political socialization has on the later behavior of the individual who is socialized. By extension this suggests an even more fundamental question about which

---

and (2) the degree to which learning is conscious and intentional. As I note below in the text, "latent" has an added ambiguity since there are two quite different kinds of nonconscious learning (unconscious and "preconscious"). In practice, Almond and Pye use "manifest" to designate what I have called "specifically political" socialization and "latent" to designate "politically relevant" socialization. But both types of socialization vary in the respects indicated above. In a later work with Sidney Verba, Almond maintains this usage while at the same time stressing the unintended, inadvertent quality of much specifically political learning. *The Civic Culture* (Princeton, N.J., Princeton University Press, 1963), pp. 323–30.

31. See the discussion of unconscious orientations toward authority figures in Chapter 3.

32. It is not satisfactory to assume, as Pye seems to, that political socialization *follows* "basic" socialization. Some political learning, as we shall see, takes place quite early in the preschool years. And "basic" socialization, i.e. personality development and the internalization of cultural values, continues into the adult years.

little reliable knowledge presently exists: What are the effects of the political learning process in any political system on the system itself?

It was not possible even to approach a comprehensive treatment of political learning in the study reported here. However, the foregoing statement gives a sense of the scope of political socialization and the place which the present study might occupy in a substantially larger map of political socialization in the United States and elsewhere.

THE NEW HAVEN POLITICAL SOCIALIZATION STUDY

The major sources of my observations in the chapters which follow are:

1. Responses of 659 New Haven, Connecticut, fourth through eighth grade children of widely diversified socioeconomic backgrounds to a paper-and-pencil questionnaire administered in classrooms in January, February, and March of 1958. The questionnaire dealt with specifically political information, attitudes, and interests, and more broadly with matters of potential political relevance, such as media behavior, and ego-ideals. It was worded so as to be neither too demanding for fourth graders (the youngest grade at which writing skills made a written instrument practical), nor too condescending for eighth graders.

2. Twenty loosely structured, tape-recorded interviews ranging from 30 to 90 minutes each with children of various ages and social backgrounds. Some of these were conducted in the summer of 1957 as a preparation to designing the questionnaire; others were conducted during and after the questionnaire administration period, with the child's filled-out questionnaire as an interview schedule. The latter served as a crude check on the reliability and validity of the questionnaire.

3. Extensive informal contact, during the period of pre-testing and administration, with children and their teachers. For example, after administering questionnaires, I often led class discussions

about government, politics, and current events, using the questionnaires as a stimulus to raise and answer questions.

4. Findings from the enormous, if uneven, literature on children's social development, including reports of other research
(most of it conducted since the New Haven field work) dealing
explicitly with children's political development.

Further aspects of the methodology of this study are discussed
in Appendix B and later in the text, where appropriate. The design
of the study, which deals with *selected* aspects of early political
learning, was influenced by the technical restraints on one-man
exploratory research, and by the paucity of directly relevant literature. At the time of the New Haven field work there were no
published data on grade school children which had been collected
with the purposes of political research explicitly in mind. Therefore, it was necessary to embark on a search for norms, for estimates
of the basic parameters of political development. It was evident
that certain variables were worth studying; for example, the development with age of the sorts of political orientations shown
to be important in adult populations. But—except in a few instances—there were insufficient background data in the literature
to begin by rigorously stating and testing hypotheses.

The case study in political learning reported in Chapter 2
provides an informal picture of how children view politics, thus
setting the stage for the discussion of quantitative findings in the
later chapters. There we consider the following problems out of
the vast universe of possible research into children's political
development:

How do children (or, at least, my sample of New Haven
children) feel about political authority? Is the initial orientation
toward politics favorable, unfavorable, or neutral? (Chapter 3)

How does information about politics develop? How do partisan
motivations develop? Is the nature and sequence of political learning significant? (Chapter 4)

How do children of high and low socioeconomic status differ
in political development? (Chapter 5)

How do boys and girls differ? (Chapter 6)

Has the content of political learning changed over the years in the United States? (Chapter 7)

What needs to be done in the way of research on children's political development, both as suggested by the New Haven findings and more generally? (Chapter 8)

CHAPTER 2

A Case Study in Early Political Learning

I interviewed Judith, a slim, alert, pony-tailed, ten-and-a-half-year-old, in July of 1957. The Suez crisis was dying out but its aftermath still occasionally reached the front pages of the newspapers; locally, the press was speculating about nominations for the coming city elections; eight months earlier, Eisenhower had been elected for his second term.

Judith is a somewhat better than average student. She lives in a modest, middle-class neighborhood. (Her father owns and operates a small hardware store.) She chatted easily, sitting with me in a vacant classroom of the school where she was attending summer classes. The tape recorder between us, although an object of curiosity, did not seem to inhibit her.

The purpose of this series of interviews was to provide me with background to design a questionnaire. Therefore, the format was loose and unstructured; I recited a series of political terms and encouraged her to tell me what she knew, thought, or felt about them.

INTERVIEWER: What do you think of when I talk about the President of the United States? What does it make you think of?

JUDITH: Well, mostly of the election, but . . . Well, thinking of President Eisenhower, I thought about when he had his heart attack and how scared everybody was.

I: Why were they scared?

J: Well, if the President died that would mean a lot of—uh—ceremony and everything—who wants the President to die? And then Nixon would take over.

I: What do you think of Nixon?

J: Ooh, mmh—he's not so hot (giggle).

I: What have you heard about him?

J: Well, he's Republican of course. And, well—do you mean politics, or just stuff like—he has a wife, and . . .

I: Either, either one.

J: Well, he has a wife (laughs). And she was with him when—on the television. And I think . . . he's in his very early forties or late thirties, I'm not sure. Isn't it you have to be over 35 to be president?

I: Uh huh.

J: Yes, I thought so.

I: Back to Eisenhower for a second—do you think of any other things, or have any particular feelings about him?

J: Well, he's always full of fun—with his golf. And I read in a magazine once that with his golf he's won more games than—I forgot his name—well, he's a champion. . . .

I: Do you have any feelings about President Eisenhower, the way he does his job or . . .

J: Well, I really don't know much about that. Really, mostly the grown-ups that know about that—the taxes and all those things about life but . . . Really, I don't know anything about that.

I: Sure. How about Adlai Stevenson? Do you think of anything particular when I mention his name?

J: Well, Stevenson was Democratic and he was a (pause) well, he put up a good fight for president, and he made good speeches. And in school we had elections on the same day and so I was the president of the Democratic team—there were four people; and so we each had to make a speech. And so it just turned out that there were more children that were Republican in the room than there were Democratic. And there was this boy—his name was R.—and he was very, very smart, and he was the president, and was just a . . . he could be the President of the United States—I'm not kidding either, he was very smart and he knew everything about this. And so he put up a good fight and so of course we lost.

I: Oh, he was on the other side.

J: Yeah, Republican.

I: What kind of things did you say on your side?

J: Oh, I don't remember. We told about the things that the Republicans can do and the Democrats . . . I mean the Republicans *can't* do and the Democrats *can*. And all different things like that. I got my speech out of a speech book that we had at home. It was one of the speeches that one of the Democratic presidents made, I forgot who it was.

I: When you think about the Republican and Democratic parties, do you think of any particular differences between them?

J: Well, some of them have different ways, like the way they want to run the country. Like President Eisenhower didn't want war, and I think Stevenson wanted to—well, not war, but he wanted to get it over with, he wanted to see what would happen. And Eisenhower wanted to get out and stop it right away.

I: Uh huh. What war was this, do you know?

J: It was with the Suez Canal and the Middle East.

I: You remember any other differences offhand between them?

J: I don't think so.

I: What do you think of when I say "the Mayor of New Haven"?

J: Well . . . hard work for him.

I: What kinds of work would you say that he does?

J: Well, he has to straighten up things . . . and by the way . . . [She continues with a rambling story about how, on the way to the beach with a neighbor, she had passed through the demolition area of the Oak Street Redevelopment Project, part of a massive urban redevelopment program for which the mayor had received considerable publicity. She is quite unaware of the details of the project and its sponsorship, although she evidently connects it with the mayor. Her main interest is in the physical impression left by the demolition, on which she dwells at length.]

I: We were talking about the mayor of New Haven. Do you know who he is?

J: Richard C. Lee.

I: What do you think about Richard C. Lee?

J: Well, he's very nice. He happens to be sort of a personal friend of my father's. And my mother is a teacher, so she met him in school when he visited the school. [At one point, Lee attempted to visit every classroom in the city annually.] So she had a long conversation with him, telling him about her children and everything. I have a sister going to college and she got a scholarship to college and so at the [high school] graduation he was giving out the diplomas, so he promised my mother he'd shake her hand and congratulate her at the graduation.

I: Did he do it?

J: Yes. [Discusses her sister; her own desire to study at the local teachers' college; and explains that her father's friendship with Mayor Lee resulted from the mayor's occasional patronage of her father's store.]

I: Back to Mayor Lee, before we pass him, do you have any feelings about him either way?

J: Well (pause), I don't know what you mean. (Laughs)

I: Well, by feelings I mean do you think he's good, bad, or indifferent, or don't you think . . .

J: Well, I really don't know the difference because I don't know too much about him.

I: What do you think of when I say "the City Hall"? Does that make you think of any particular things that go on?

J: Polio shots (laughs). That's where I got my polio shot; down in the basement.

I: Can you think of any other things that go on in the building?

J: Well, where they . . . There's a big sign there that says "taxes" and I always wanted to know what that meant. It has a finger pointing to where to go, so one day I went strolling down there to see what was happening, but it was closed.

I: Did you ever find out what it meant?

J: No, I was going to ask my father, but I never got to it.

I: Do you know what taxes are?

J: Well, like . . . use of everything. You have to pay for the children to go to school . . . use of roads like the toll house, and all different things.

I: You know what a tax is, don't you, but . . .

J: Yes.

I: But you just don't know what it means when you see a sign that says "taxes" with a finger pointing.

J: Well, I know what it means where . . . ah . . . I know what "taxes" means, do they just go there and pay their taxes, or send it in, or what?

I: What do you think of if I say the governor of Connecticut?

J: Well, I really don't know much about that.

I: Have you heard about that job?

J: Isn't it Ribicoff?

I: Yes, that's right. Do you know anything about him?

J: No. (Laughs) All I know is my neighbor's crazy about him . . . she's very mixed in with . . . with politics. So she has to watch television and nobody can make a sound while he's on or making a speech or something.

I: Why does she like him? Did she ever tell you?

J: Ahh . . . I don't know. [She is unable to name other state officials, such as the party leaders.]

I: How about Albert Cretella [then the incumbent congressman from the third congressional district of Connecticut], who's he?

J: Oh yes, well (laughs) let's see, isn't he . . . I'm not sure. I always got him mixed up with someone else . . . he's with the politics too . . . Let me see, was he . . . I think he was . . . was he a Republican? I think so. Was he?

I: I'm not supposed to tell you.

J: (Laughs.) I'm not sure. *Was* he?

I: Yeah.

J: (Laughs.) Yes, I thought so.

I: Do you have any opinion about him?

J: Well, no. All I know is we're not Republicans. My father isn't.

I: Have you ever heard about Prescott Bush [then Connecticut's senior senator]?

J: Yes.

I: What have you heard?

J: I think he's Republican too . . . I don't remember . . . Yes, he's a Republican too.

I: What's his job?

J: (Pause.) I'm not sure.

I: Have you ever heard of the Congress?

J: Yes.

I: Where is that, or what does it do?

J: Isn't it in Washington? And I'm not too sure of what it does . . . About all the laws that have to go through Congress, through different stages to become a law.

I: Can you think of any particular laws . . .

J: (Laughs.) I don't think so.

I: How about the Connecticut General Assembly [the state legislature]? Does that sound familiar?

J: I don't think so.

I: How about the word "elections"? What does it make you think of?

J: The elections? Well, where you nominate, ah, the, elections for president; in our classrooms, or a woman's club, or anything like that. Where you have to elect a president, vice president, secretary, treasurer, anything in that line.

I: Can you remember any elections that interested you or that you were involved with in some way?

J: Well, the election for president. They always used to have how they were going written on the board on television, so I liked to see who was winning . . . how far they were getting up.

I: You watched that during the last presidential election?

J: Yes.

I: Did you feel very interested in it at the time?

J: At the time, yes. But I knew it would be over soon and I was happy about that!

I: About the fact that it *would* be over soon?

J: Yes.

I: Why were you happy about that?

J: Well, all you saw on television was the elections, the elections, the elections (laughs).

I: Did you get tired of that?

J: Oh yes, from nine o'clock in the morning to nine at night!

I: Were you for anyone during that period?

J: Well, my father was Democratic, so we stuck to him.

I: How about this word—a politician? Do you think of anything when you hear it?

J: Well, that's a person who's in politics.

I: Uh huh. For instance, what kinds of people can you think of?

J: The President's in politics! And Richard Nixon, the Vice President, and Richard [*sic*] Dulles, the Secretary of State, and so on. . . .

I: How about when I say "the government"? Does that make you think of any particular things?

J: Well, the government is really what runs the whole United States, or the state, or the country.

I: How about this word? Have you ever heard the word "bribe" used?

J: Bribe? Well, I don't know if this is what it means, but . . . like to bribe somebody to do something . . . push them into it . . . sort of get them to do it.

I: How about the word "democracy," what does that mean?

J: Democracy . . . oh. Well, democracy is really a kind of—well, what the people have—well, I can't explain it!

I: Say the words that come to your mind.

J: Well, democracy is sort of what the people should have . . . well, you should have democracy and be . . . well, it's like . . . uh!

I: You're not exactly sure what it is?

J: I'm not exactly sure but in a way I am—it's what the people should have, they should have democracy, like be a good citizen, or something like that—I can't explain it.

I: Uh huh—it's something good at any rate.

J: Yes.

I: You're not completely sure about the details.

J: No, I'm not.

I: Did I ask you what sorts of things you thought of when you heard the word "communism"?

J: Communism? No, you didn't.

I: What does it mean to you offhand?

J: Well, communism is sort of—it's a different way of people; well, sort of like . . . to me it's *bad.* I can't explain it, just like democracy—it's sort of the opposite.

No interview is typical. Judith's has much in common with the quantitative findings from the larger sample as they apply to children of similar characteristics: girls, middle-class children, the middle age groups in the sample. The reader might well return to this interview after completing the remaining chapters. Without anticipating the findings reported there in any detail, we may simply note that a number of Judith's remarks do provide illustrations of observations which will be discussed in the remainder of the book. In her descriptions, for example, of Eisenhower, Stevenson, and Mayor Lee and in her unfamiliarity with terms such as "bribe," we get a sense of the feeling-tone of her fragmentary impressions of politics and politicians, a topic we deal with in Chapter 3. The portions of my conversation with her concerning Congressmen and dealing with her—and her father's—preference for the Democratic party illustrate points made in Chapter 4 about the nature of early political information and the childhood antecedents of adult partisanship. She stands in contrast to the far less articulate and less open lower-class children who will be discussed in Chapter 5, and she also illustrates certain of the findings about childhood political sex differences discussed in Chapter 6. Above all, Judith provides us with some sense of the buzzing, blooming reality from which the statistics and analytic categories are abstracted.

CHAPTER 3

Children's Feelings about Political Authority

Citizens' feelings about political authority have a complex and imperfectly understood, but important, bearing on the equilibrium of the body politic. People inevitably have assumptions about their leaders: assumptions about whether leaders are benign or malignant, whether they are on a plane with "the rest of us" or whether they are a higher order of being. These assumptions probably vary from one leadership role to another, and within and between societies. In this chapter we shall examine their childhood antecedents.

The feelings New Haven children displayed toward political authority were striking. In some respects they resembled adult political views; in others they were distinctively childlike. Their childlike aspect was sufficiently pervasive to be elicited unexpectedly by a research procedure not primarily designed to deal with feelings toward authority. Before discussing the New Haven findings we might usefully consider *adult* feelings about political authority.

ADULT AMBIVALENCE TOWARD POLITICAL AUTHORITY

Adult assessments of political leaders are curiously inconsistent. In some ways Americans seem to have an abiding distrust of politics and politicians. For example, more Americans agree than disagree with statements such as "it is almost impossible for a man to stay honest if he goes into politics," a substantial proportion of the population feels that it is at best dubious for a young man to make politics his career, and similar anti-politician attitudes often are elicited by public opinion polls. Cynical, unsympathetic images of politics and the politician also are revealed by a great many adults in responses to various questions about the individual's political efficacy, as measured for example by willingness to agree with the statement "I don't think public officials care much what people like me think."[1]

But this is not the whole story. Other studies have shown that Americans hold specific political roles—for example, senator, mayor, and governor—in exceedingly *high* esteem. Over the years, the many studies of occupational prestige have shown that people rank these roles well above all but an occasional civilian role such as physician in terms of importance and status.[2] These inconsistencies led one commentator to write of "the ambivalent social status of the American politician."[3]

Public responses to individual politicians fluctuate greatly. Perhaps the best barometer of this variation is the American Institute of Public Opinion's regular estimates of presidential popularity. Since the 1930s, countless national cross-sections have been asked, "Do you approve or disapprove of the way President X has been

1. H. Cantril and M. Strunk, *Public Opinion: 1935–1946* (Princeton, Princeton University Press, 1951), p. 584; National Opinion Research Center, *The Public Looks at Politics and Politicians* (Report No. 20, March 1944); Angus Campbell et al., *The Voter Decides* (Evanston, Row, Peterson, 1954), pp. 187–94. Also see Robert E. Agger et al., "Political Cynicism: Measurement and Meaning," *Journal of Politics, 23* (1961), 477–506, and Edgar Litt, "Political Cynicism and Political Futility," ibid., *25* (1963), 312–23.

2. See "Jobs and Occupations: A Popular Evaluation," *Opinion News, 9* (September 1, 1949), 3–19; Mapheus Smith, "An Empirical Scale of Prestige Status of Occupations," *American Sociological Review, 8* (1943), 185–92; Harvey C. Lehman and Paul A. Witty, "Further Study of the Social Status of Occupations," *The Journal of Educational Sociology, 5* (1931–32); George W. Hartmann, "The Prestige of Occupations," *The Personnel Journal, 13* (1934–35), 144–52. For an early attempt at cross-cultural study, see Jerome Davis, "Testing the Social Attitudes of Children in the Government Schools in Russia," *American Journal of Sociology, 32* (1926–27), 947–52.

3. William C. Mitchell, in the *Western Political Quarterly, 12* (1959), 683–98.

handling his job?" Favorable response to Roosevelt, during his term in office, ranged from 50 per cent to 84 per cent; approval of Truman from 23 per cent to 87 per cent; Eisenhower from 49 per cent to 79 per cent. Support for Kennedy, although consistently high during his administration, also was variable, ranging from a low of 57 per cent to a high of 83 per cent.[4]

One of the most substantial assets of the president evidently is the public respect for his role and his symbolic position at the pinnacle of the nation. Thus it has been shown that the mere fact of incumbency is sufficient to improve a leader's reputation with people who had previously been skeptical of him. One study of this tendency elicited statements like the following, made several weeks after the 1952 election by a Stevenson supporter who had been critical of Eisenhower: "I feel a little more confident in his ability as a president. The change . . . is probably due only to the reason that he has been elected president. I can't explain myself too well, but I feel that Eisenhower is just a better man than I had imagined."[5] When a vice-president assumes the presidency unexpectedly, after the death in office of a president, this effect may be especially visible, as can be seen from the

4. For a summary of trends in the public support of Roosevelt, Truman, and Eisenhower see the poll findings reported by Helen Gaudet Erskine in *Public Opinion Quarterly*, 25 (1961), 135–37. Data on Kennedy's popularity may be found in subsequent installments of Mrs. Erskine's regular reports of the polls in *ibid.* and in the regular news releases of The American Institute of Public Opinion, especially the November 10 and December 15, 1963 releases.

5. I. H. Paul, "Impressions of Personality, Authoritarianism, and the *Fait Accompli* Effect," *Journal of Abnormal and Social Psychology*, 53 (1956), 343. Also see Hadley Cantril, *Gauging Public Opinion* (Princeton, Princeton University Press, 1944), pp. 37–38; Paul F. Lazarsfeld et al., *The People's Choice* (New York, Columbia University Press, 1944), pp. 37–38; Paul F. Lazarsfeld, "Public Opinion and the Classical Tradition," *Public Opinion Quarterly*, 21 (1957), 47; and V. O. Key, Jr., *Public Opinion and American Democracy* (New York, Knopf, 1961), p. 479. This seems to be a part of a more general phenomenon which has been called the *fait accompli* effect. For example, support for a bill increases after it has been passed and becomes a law and, conversely, people are less likely to support a policy if they are told it will be necessary to change a law or amend the Constitution to attain this goal.

following interviews conducted in the immediate aftermath of President Kennedy's assassination.[6]

In 1960 I came to the conclusion on the basis of very little evidence that [Lyndon Johnson] was a megalomaniac and somebody I didn't want to see in the White House. . . . I thought . . . he really wanted to hold complete power over government in his hands. . . . Immediately upon hearing that Kennedy died, I started revising my opinion and got much more temperate. . . . In about five minutes . . . I just decided that, well, you know, he's really a great tactician and we have to give him a chance and all we can do is hope for the best.

We immediately began to think of Johnson in slightly better terms than we [had] before.

Just the fact that he was in the presidency gave him a sort of deification.

I thought [after hearing of President Kennedy's assassination], "Oh my God, what are we going to do with Johnson in there?" And then I thought and thought. Well, gee, I was kind of impressed a little earlier with him, you know, before he was vice-president I didn't think he was such a bad guy. Maybe things aren't going to be so bad after all.

The polls have generally shown a rise in the post-election popularity of reelected incumbents. They also show the striking willingness of citizens to rally around the president when his role of national leader in the international arena is emphasized— for example, during Roosevelt's period of wartime leadership, after the dispatch of troops to Korea by Truman and to Lebanon

6. Fred I. Greenstein, "College Student Reactions to the Assassination of President Kennedy," paper delivered at Conference on Children's Reactions to the Death of the President, April 1964; to be published in abbreviated form in Bradley S. Greenberg and Edwin B. Parker, eds., *Communication in Crisis* (Stanford, Stanford University Press, 1965). Nelson W. Polsby and I conducted the interviews quoted in the text.

by Eisenhower, and after Kennedy's declaration of blockade during the 1962 Cuban crisis.[7]

CHILDREN'S IDEALIZATION OF POLITICAL AUTHORITY

The most conspicuous difference between adult political orientations and those of the New Haven children was in attitudes of cynicism and distrust toward politics. Virtually *no* children entertained these widespread adult views. In spite of a variety of attempts to evoke such responses during my preliminary interviewing and pretesting, for example, the references to "politician" and "bribe" in the interview with Judith, there was no evidence even of a frame of reference which would make it possible to use questionnaire items designed to evoke political cynicism. The final version of the New Haven questionnaire contained a number of items which might have evoked spontaneous references to the malignancy of politicians, but only one or two of the 659 children made statements which could be construed in this way. Instead, as we shall see, the spontaneous references to politicians had a remarkably benign quality.[8] We may now look more specifically at three classes of New Haven findings which bear on this: children's rankings of the "importance" of political leaders; their evaluations of the incumbent president, governor, and mayor; and their spontaneous statements.

7. See references in note 4. On Roosevelt, see Cantril and Strunk, *Public Opinion: 1935–1946*, p. 756.

8. This is not to say that children never develop aversions to *individual* political leaders, although as is shown below, they probably are less likely than adults to do so. One item which did evoke spontaneous negative references to individual politicians asked the child, "Name a famous person you *don't* want to be like." About 15 per cent of the respondents named a political leader of the present or of the recent past. Interestingly, more than half of these references were to foreign leaders such as Nikita Khrushchev. Follow-up interviews suggested that some of the negative references to domestic leaders were rejections of the responsibility of being (say) president, rather than personal criticisms of the leader.

The importance of political leaders

New Haven children were asked to tell which of a number of
adult roles are "most important." Choices offered included the
president and mayor, authority figures of the immediate environment such as school principals and teachers, as well as physicians,
clergymen, police chiefs, and judges. *At every age level, there were
more references to the president and mayor than to any of the
other roles.* Thus, although the negative side of adult images of
politicians is not present in childhood, the positive side—the at-
tribution of great prestige to specific roles—emerges early.

How early? Table 3.1, which reports the responses of the
youngest group in this sample, shows that by the age of nine the
belief that the president and mayor are figures of great importance
is firmly entrenched. Both political executives are mentioned by
over 20 per cent more children than is the next most prestigeful
individual, the physician. Indeed, there is a clear distinction in
the data between estimates of the importance of the president and
mayor, and estimates of the importance of the other six figures.
The gap between each of the remaining roles is in no case greater
than 13 per cent.

The importance of political roles clearly is learned quite early,
before the age of nine. The age at which children first acquire
this particular evaluation cannot be determined from the New
Haven sample, but since reporting this finding in 1960, I have
learned of several instances in which children of preschool age
(in one case a two-year-old) showed a respectful awareness of the
president, and, in the Kennedy years, of the presidential family.[9]
The nine-year-olds whose responses are reported in Table 3.1
have virtually no specific *knowledge* of the presidential or mayoral
roles. Children of this age (fourth graders) were uniformly aware
of President Eisenhower's name (96 per cent could name him in

9. There have been a number of popular accounts of young children's
interest in President Kennedy and his family. For example, Bill Adler, *Kids'
Letters to President Kennedy* (New York, Morrow, 1961).

TABLE 3.1. Judgments by Fourth Grade Children of which Adult Roles are "Most Important"*

Roles	Per cent choosing each role
President	80
Mayor	79
Doctor	57
Police chief	51
Judge	48
School teacher	35
Religious leader	32
School principal	22
Number of cases	111

*Children were permitted four choices, so the percentages exceed 100. The mayor's prestige may be a function of the great personal popularity of New Haven's incumbent city executive.

the written questionnaire) and only slightly less aware (90 per cent) of the name of New Haven's popular mayor. But, using the most generous coding standards, less than a fourth of them could describe the president's duties; about a third could make a "reasonably accurate" statement about the mayor, largely because New Haven's Mayor Lee was then engaged in a spectacular and highly publicized urban renewal program. Awareness of other aspects of the political environment (e.g. the governor and the legislative bodies at various levels of government) was nil, as we shall see when considering the development of cognitive information in Chapter 4.

The following passage from an interview with a seven-year-old (just beginning second grade) provides some insight into the character of young children's conceptions of political leaders:

INTERVIEWER: Have you ever heard of the President of the United States?

ROBERT: Yes.

I: What is his name?

R: Eisenhower.

I: What does he do?

R: Well, sometimes he . . . well, you know . . . a lot of times when people go away he'll say goodbye and he's on programs and they do work.

I: What kind of work does he do? Do you know any more about it?

R: (After thought) Studying.

I: What sorts of things does he study?

R: Like things they gotta do . . . like important . . . what's happening and the weather and all that.

I: Now tell me this. Who is more important, the President of the United States or a doctor?

R: (Pause) The President.

I: Who do you think is more important, the President of the United States or a school teacher?

R: (Emphatically) President!

I: Why is the president more important?

R: They do much more work and they're much importanter. School teacher isn't.

I: (After being told in response to further questions that the president also is more important than a storekeeper and than a general in the army): Who do you think is more important than the president?

R: (Long pause) Lemme see . . . I don't know.

Robert is unshakable in his assessment of the president's importance. He has acquired this assessment—as his attempt to explain the president's duties in terms of a workaday seven-year-old frame of reference shows—in the absence of even a moderately precise awareness of what the president does. The exact reason for the president's importance is one of those adult mysteries which, like the daily weather forecast, appear on the television screen in the intervals between broadcasts for children. If the president is important, he *must* do important things, as does Robert's older brother, who studies his homework.

Evaluations and "affective knowledge" about political leaders precede the factual information on which one might assume they would be based. In the next chapter we shall examine a quite similar pattern of development, the genesis of identification with political parties. Here also, the emotional tie to an aspect of the adult political world precedes even moderately differentiated cognitive development. Political information increases substantially over the brief age span of the New Haven sample, but the structure of factual knowledge is erected on a foundation of feelings, assessments, and opinions.

Evaluations of public officials

Another point at which children's orientations can be compared, at least crudely, with adult responses is in ratings of individual political leaders. Following the various information items which called, for example, for descriptions of the mayor, governor, and president, the children were asked to evaluate these leaders on a four-point scale ranging from "very good" to "bad."

Here children's responses did not merely reflect what might be expected from comparable adult samples. Their modal assessment of each of the three incumbents was in the highest possible category—"very good."[10] The New Haven survey was conducted during the period of national soul-searching which followed the long-delayed American response to the first Russian space satellite launching. Judging from the way national cross-sections of adults responded to the opportunity to rate President Eisenhower during this period, *children's views of political leaders are substantially*

10. For a discussion of the validity of the responses reported in Table 3.2 see Fred I. Greenstein, "The Benevolent Leader: Children's Images of Political Authority," *American Political Science Review*, 54 (1960), 937 n.

more favorable than those of their elders. Table 3.2 contrasts the
New Haven responses with the American Institute of Public
Opinion's February 1958 report of the president's popularity.
Needless to say, this comparison of New Haven findings with
national survey data must be treated as suggestive;[11] however,
differences between adults and children in evaluation of the president are considerable. Adults were about five times more willing
to criticize the chief executive. It is only during the immediately
post-election honeymoon periods that the AIPO finds as few as
five per cent of the adult population critical of the president.[12]

New Haven responses to items dealing with political efficacy
also suggest that children are far more positive in their political
orientations than adults. Less than two per cent of the children
said that they would not vote when they reached twenty-one. And
over two thirds agreed that "it makes much difference who wins
an election," in contrast to the markedly smaller proportions of
adult samples making such statements.[13]

11. At least three points of noncomparability should be noted: the differences in population (New Haven versus a National sample); the differences
in question wording; and the differences in response alternatives. With these
major reservations in mind, the following additional AIPO findings on President Eisenhower, for the months surrounding this survey, may be noted.
(AIPO releases November 1957, January and March 1958.)

	Approve	Disapprove	No Opinion
November 1957	57%	27%	16%
January 1958	60	30	10
March 1958	52	33	15

The November AIPO report, which controls for region, suggests that Southern
responses may have inflated the "disapproval" column. In that month, Eastern
states were reported as 65% approve, 21% disapprove, and 14% no opinion.
This still is considerably more than the 5% of the New Haven children who
checked the "bad" and "not very good" alternatives.

12. See notes 4 and 7. In Germany, expressions of disapproval of Adenauer
never fell below 15 per cent between 1949 and 1962. Erich P. Newmann and
Elisabeth Noelle, *Statistics on Adenauer* (Allensbach and Bonn, Verlag für
Demoskopie, 1962), pp. 40–44.

13. For example, in the Survey Research Center's 1952 election study
sample, only a fifth of the respondents claimed that "it would make a great
deal of difference to the country whether the Democrats or the Republicans

TABLE 3.2. Children's Evaluations of Three Political Executives Contrasted with Adult Evaluations of President Eisenhower during the Same Time Period

	Children				*Adults[a]*
	Mayor	*Governor*	*President*		*President*
Very good	62%	40%	71%	Approve	58%
Fairly good	27	28	21		
Not very good	4	2	4	Disapprove	27
Bad	1	—[b]	1		
Don't know	6	30	4	No opinion	15
Number of cases	651[c]	643[c]	649[c]		

a. February 1958 AIPO findings, reported in March 1958 release. These findings are based on a national sample. On their comparability with the New Haven data, see footnote 11.

b. Less than 1 per cent.

c. Number of cases does not equal complete sample due to invalid responses.

The benevolence of leaders

I have already noted that various items in the New Haven questionnaire might have stimulated spontaneous references to graft, corruption, and political immorality, if these images were important in children's perceptions of politics. References of this sort were not made. Instead a quite different set of images emerged spontaneously in response to the six open-ended items asking for descriptions of the duties of local, state, and federal executives and legislative bodies. The items were quite unstructured, simply

---

win the elections." Campbell et al., *The Voter Decides,* p. 38. The same reservations about comparability of samples, question wording, and response alternatives expressed in note 11, above, are also relevant here.

The Survey Research Center reports that 43 per cent of the respondents replied "some difference, minor differences." Compare a 1946 cross-section of the national population which was asked: "Do you think it makes much difference or only a little difference which party wins the elections for Congress this fall?" About half said it made "much difference," about 30 per cent "little," and the remaining 20 per cent was divided evenly between "no difference" and "no opinion." Cantril and Strunk, p. 582.

asking, "What sorts of things does the mayor (etc.) do?" As might be expected, most of the children who were able to respond made rather straightforward factual assertions—"The mayor runs the city"; "Congress makes laws"; etc. What was surprising, however, was that a conspicuous minority of the children volunteered affective or affectively toned responses—especially in descriptions of the mayor and president. As noted above, only one or two of these statements were unsympathetic. Several classes of response are worth examining.

SERVICES TO CHILDREN. About ten per cent of the responses to the mayor were to child-related portions of his role. For example:

> The mayor makes parks and swings. (Fifth grade girl.)
> The mayor repairs the parks, roads, schools, and takes the snow off the roads when it snows. (Fifth grade boy.)

It is a reasonable assumption that when a child's first image of a political leader emphasizes pork-barrel indulgences to the child, the image is favorable.

NORMATIVE ROLE. In addition, some children explicitly characterized political leaders in positive normative terms—either as people "who do good things," or as specialists in making moral judgments:

> The president does good work. (Sixth grade boy.)

> The mayor sends men to build parks for us and make our city be a good one. (Fourth grade girl.)

> The president makes peace with every country but bad. (Fifth grade boy.)

> The mayor talks business to all the people and says what's wrong or bad. (Fourth grade girl.)

> I think that he [the president] has the right to stop bad things before they start. (Fifth grade girl.)

GENERAL BENEVOLENCE. More generally, children tended to describe political leaders as "helping," "taking care of," and "protecting" people. Benevolent perceptions of this sort were especially evident in descriptions of the president and mayor, but also occasionally were apparent in descriptions of the governor and of legislative bodies. For example:

> The president deals with foreign countries and takes care of the U.S. (Eighth grade boy.)

> The mayor helps people to live in safety. . . . The president is doing a very good job of making people be safe. (Fourth grade girl.)

> The president gives us freedom. (Eighth grade girl.)

> The Board of Aldermen gives us needs so we could live well. (Fourth grade girl.)

In a few cases children went so far as to perceive political authority as a direct source of economic support:

> The mayor pays working people like banks. (Fifth grade boy.)

> The mayor sees that schools have what they need and stores and other places too. (Fifth grade girl.)

> The mayor helps everyone to have nice homes and jobs. (Fourth grade boy.)

The frequency of references to the mayor connected with services to children and of generally "benevolent" and "normative" references to the mayor and president is shown in Table 3.3. Here we see that statements of this sort were made by some children at every age level, but that benevolent imagery declines with age. Although the total of these classes of response rarely exceeds 15 per cent in any cell of Table 3.3, what is remarkable is that any such images are expressed in answer to such bland, unstructured stimulus questions. Moreover, additional descriptions of political leaders had favorable connotations which do not fit as

TABLE 3.3. Children's Images of the Mayor and President, by School Year*

	School Year				
	4th	5th	6th	7th	8th
Mayor					
Benevolence: "helps us" "gives us freedom"	20%	16%	9%	3%	4%
Normative role: "does good things" "tells what is right or wrong"	7	12	13	8	12
Services to children: "makes parks and swings"	15	14	1	11	15
Number of cases	55	82	98	115	151
President					
Benevolence	26%	11%	5%	5%	4%
Normative	5	9	11	3	7
Number of cases	62	80	95	112	160

*Percentages are based on those children who were able to produce a description of the executive role, whether or not the description was "reasonably accurate" (excluding grossly inaccurate or vague statements).

readily into a few simple categories. For example, some children placed emphasis on the wisdom, capability, and solicitousness of public officials:

> The president is in charge of the United States and has many wise men to tell him what is best. (Sixth grade boy.)

> The president worries about all the problems of all the 48 states. Takes care of threatening wars by holding peace conferences. (Seventh grade boy.)

> The mayor has to keep track of everything that happens in New Haven. (Sixth grade boy.)

The spontaneous appearance of these images suggests that appropriately structured questions would show the imagery of benevolence to be considerably more common among grade school children than Table 3.3 indicates.[14]

The research of David Easton and Robert Hess makes it clear that this indeed is the case. At approximately the same time as the New Haven field work, Easton and Hess[15] studied the political socialization of 366 second through eighth grade children in a Chicago suburb. The Chicago study employed a number of multiple choice items specifically designed to detect idealization of authority: for example, questions asking whether the president is "the best person in the world," "a good person," or "not a good person." The findings clearly demonstrated idealization of the president by young children, and a rather complicated pattern of deidealization with age, depending upon the facet of the presidential image referred to by the child. Thus, 60 per cent of the second graders and only two per cent of the eighth graders took the hyperbolic position that the president was "the best person in the world." About three quarters of the second graders and less than half of the eighth graders agreed that the president "likes almost

14. Another class of political imagery is worth noting. A small percentage of the respondents (but some in each of the four schools which make up the sample) coped with the problem of organizing their fragmentary political information by using hierarchical concepts. They saw politics, even in the case of individuals and institutions which are formally coordinate, in terms of a chain of command. For example: "The mayor gets orders from the president . . . The president gives orders to the governor." (Fifth grade girl.) "The mayor handles the minor problems and if it is too big he goes to the governor." (Seventh grade boy.) "The mayor takes the problems of the town. He [the governor] takes the hard problems." (Fifth grade boy.) One notably ingenious misconception combined hierarchy with benevolence. The fifth grade boy whose statement that "The mayor pays working people like banks" was cited above went on to say, "The governor pays mayors. . . . The president pays the governor." Again the appropriate instrument might reveal that this way of perceiving politics is reasonably common in childhood and, perhaps, that it is related to certain types of nonpolitical—e.g. primary group—experiences. See note 34, below.

15. Robert D. Hess and David Easton, "The Child's Image of the President," *Public Opinion Quarterly*, 24 (1960), 632–44. For a comparison of this work with certain of the New Haven findings see Fred I. Greenstein, "More on Children's Images of the President," *Public Opinion Quarterly*, 25 (1961), 648–54.

everybody." Comparisons of other attributes of the president with "most men" (e.g. his knowledge, "how hard" he works) also produced highly favorable responses, but in these cases the responses did not decrease—some even increased slightly—with age. A replication by Easton and Hess shortly after Kennedy's inauguration demonstrated that the findings were not simply a function of Eisenhower's incumbency; additional studies in other nations (Chile, Puerto Rico, Australia, and Japan) showed tendencies, which parallel the New Haven findings, for young children to perceive political leaders as benevolent, and for the leader's image to lose some of this positive coloration among older children.[16]

The New Haven findings may be summarized as follows: (1) children are at least as likely as adults to perceive high political roles as being important; (2) they seem to be more sympathetic to individual political leaders (and, in general, to politics) than are adults; (3) in at least some cases their actual images of political leaders are qualitatively different from the images one would expect adults to hold, especially in the emphasis on benignness; and (4), most important, the widespread adult political cynicism and distrust do not seem to have developed by eighth grade (age 13).

CAUSES AND CONSEQUENCES OF THE CHILD'S VIEW OF POLITICAL AUTHORITY

Why is the child's early view of political authority so strikingly favorable? What, if any, effect does this aspect of individual political development have on adult political behavior and on the

---

16. Robert D. Hess, "The Socialization of Attitudes Toward Political Authority: Some Crossnational Comparisons," *International Social Science Journal, 15* (1963), 542–59. There are interesting variations from nation to nation in the absolute levels of idealization, but the tendency for younger children to display more idealized conceptions of leaders than do older children is consistent from nation to nation. Also see Daniel Rosenblatt's finding that American adults were more likely than a matched sample of Russians "to view the father as . . . wise and benevolent." "Responses of Former Soviet Citizens to Selected *TAT* Cards," *Journal of General Psychology, 62* (1960), 278.

political system? Fully convincing answers to this pair of questions (particularly the second) are not available. This is so partly because the New Haven data are limited, but also because the existing body of basic knowledge linking childhood experience and adult behavior is quite rudimentary,[17] as is our understanding of the connections between individual attitudes and behavior and the functioning of political systems.

Sources of the child's view of authority

In hypothesizing about how children acquire their idealized conceptions of political authority, it is important (as was suggested in Chapter 1) to consider not only the agencies of socialization to which children are exposed, but also the socialized themselves —what children "are able to absorb and what they selectively perceive and misperceive."[18]

As with a number of other aspects of political learning we shall consider, conceptions of leaders seem to spring up in a singularly haphazard manner. In New Haven, at least, there is little formal adult effort to shape the political information and attitudes of grade school children. No mandatory provision for training in the subject matter once called civics exists until eighth grade. Social studies curriculum guides do not even suggest the possibility of introducing such training until sixth grade. New Haven is not unique in this respect, judging from the following report on social studies teaching:

> In most cases, the social studies program of the primary grades (K-3) focuses on the home, family, and community. In the intermediate grades, children usually study about their home states, about the United States, about some foreign countries, and sometimes about the history of the Old World. In grades seven and eight, geography or community study and the study of the U.S.A. are the general rule. Ex-

17. For a summary of this literature, see Irvin L. Child, "Socialization," in Lindzey, ed., *Handbook of Social Psychology*, 2, 655–92.
18. See p. 12 above.

amination of materials used throughout these grades, especially in K-4, shows that study of politics and government,
when included, is often incidental rather than central.[19]

The children themselves, with very rare exceptions, do not actively search for political information; at the younger age levels in
the sample, in fact, few interests are evident beyond the child's
immediate circle.

Nevertheless, by adolescence a large proportion of the political
orientations which guide the participation of adult voters are already present. Many of these orientations are acquired during the
fourth through eighth grade years covered by the New Haven
study; a few, including the perception—in an idealized form—
of leaders such as the president, are already evident by fourth
grade.

The most important source of children's conceptions of authority undoubtedly is the civic instruction which goes on incidental
to normal activities in the family.[20] Children overhear parental
conversations; they sense, or are informally told of, their parents'
stance toward political authority in general and partisan politics
in particular. Parents are called upon to answer questions about
politics just as they are called upon to answer questions about the
thousand and one other aspects of society the child gradually becomes aware of. Inadvertent political learning also takes place in
the schools; patriotic rituals are observed, national heroes (including Washington and Lincoln) are discussed, and, during election
campaigns, partisanship, campaign buttons, and the general bally-
hoo of American elections spill over not only into the classroom,
but also into the peer-group, neighborhood, and—especially—
the mass media, as we saw in Judith's lament about election
broadcasting.[21] Between as well as during elections, the mass

19. Gloria Cammarota, "Children, Politics, and Elementary Social Studies,"
Social Education, 27 (1963), 205. Also see Robert D. Hess and David Easton,
"The Role of the Elementary School in Political Socialization," *The School
Review,* 70 (1962), 257–65.

20. Cf. Hyman, *Political Socialization,* Chap. 4.

21. See p. 24 above.

media seem to be especially important agents of informal learning.[22] Children only rarely attend closely to political news (although dramatic political events, such as satellite launchings and integration crises, *do* interest children deeply). But they inevitably are exposed to reports of the adult political world and willy-nilly a rough conception of politics begins to form.[23]

There are a number of possible reasons for the peculiarly idealized character of early political images. One is the nature of the political communications adults direct to children. While there is no explicit norm in the United States that children should be "protected" from politics, it is likely that adults—even politically cynical adults—more or less unconsciously sugarcoat the political explanations they pass on to children. As Easton and Hess have suggested,[24] politics may be in the same class as sex—one of

22. Cf. Fred I. Greenstein, "Children's Political Perspectives: A Study of the Development of Political Awareness and Preferences among Preadolescents" (unpublished Ph.D. dissertation, Yale University Library, 1959) for data on the political aspects of children's media behavior.

Iona and Peter Opie observe, somewhat wistfully, that English school children "undoubtedly . . . were more actively employed in nineteenth-century parliamentary elections than they are today. . . . Election time . . . used to be, and still is in the United States, a period of high spirits . . ." They record two bits of juvenile political rhyme from the Roosevelt–Willkie campaign:

> Fried cats
> And stewed rats
> Are good enough
> For the Democrats.

> Roosevelt in the White House
> Waited to be elected;
> Willkie in the garbage can
> Waiting to be collected.

The Lore and Language of School Children (Oxford, Oxford University Press, 1959), pp. 348–49.

23. For the suggestion that inadvertent political learning of the sort discussed here "is more significant than . . . formal education" because "the child hears informally . . . the real political attitudes of adults" see Gabriel A. Almond and Sidney Verba, *The Civic Culture,* pp. 325–26 and 498–99.

24. David Easton and Robert D. Hess, "The Child's Political World," *Midwest Journal of Political Science,* 6 (1962), 229–46.

those sordid aspects of adult existence from which it is thought that young children are best shielded.

What young children are "willing" to learn is probably as important as what adults are willing to teach. Parents, teachers, and the very setting of childhood (especially dependency upon adults) provide children with something considerably more important than specific political attitudes—namely, general orientations to the adult world. Through the entirety of his experiences with adults the child acquires a frame of reference within which to place an especially important class of adult—the political leader. Having learned to see adults many times larger than life size, children are likely simply to misperceive and otherwise screen out discordant information about "corruption" and other negative aspects of the adult political environment.[25] Since it is not possible that children are completely insulated from adult attitudes of distrust toward politics, selective perception of this sort would seem to be an important explanation of the lack of political cynicism among children.

Psychoanalytic theory suggests another and deeper way in which experiences with authority figures in the immediate environment may affect responses to authority in the wider political world. Figures in the latter setting, for instance the president, are *unconsciously* (i.e. in a way not accessible to conscious awareness) perceived as the analogues of parents and other immediate environment authorities. The public figure becomes invested with powerful private feelings; response to him assumes some of the qualities of response to family members and others in the face-to-face environment.

25. An added element contributing to these perceptions of adults undoubtedly is the painfully benevolent portrayal of the wider environment in contemporary children's literature. Books such as *Our Friend the Farmer* and *How the Policeman Helps Us* are couched in language which closely resembles some of the preadolescent descriptions of political leaders reported above. Cf. Martin Mayer, *The Schools* (New York, Anchor Books, 1963), p. 378. Nineteenth-century children's literature evidently presented the world in far less sanguine terms. See *The* [London] *Times Literary Supplement Children's Book Section,* June 14, 1963, pp. 421–22.

This notion was first advanced to political scientists by Harold Lasswell.[26] It now is quite familiar and in fact has been thoroughly vulgarized, particularly during the Eisenhower years, in the form of popular references to political "father figures." Vulgarizations notwithstanding, there may be considerable empirical substance to the thesis that private orientations to authority become channeled into public orientations. A good bit of scattered psychiatric evidence based upon patients in therapy has accumulated.[27] Further, public behavior during certain "extreme conditions," such as the unexpected death of a popular leader, is quite consistent with the hypothesis that such an unconscious analogy exists. On these occasions, not only do many citizens experience extreme grief of the sort we expect to find when a parent has died, but they also often draw this analogy themselves. Orlansky[28] reports the following reactions to Roosevelt's death:

> You expect me to say something about what happened. But I cannot speak about Roosevelt's death any more than I could speak about the death of my mother and father. (New York high school teacher to her class.)

> It's almost as though father had died. (Liberal newspaper editor.)

26. Harold D. Lasswell, *Psychopathology and Politics,* reprinted in *The Political Writings of Harold D. Lasswell,* p. 173 f. In addition, see Lasswell's *Power and Personality* (New York, Norton, 1948), pp. 156–57, and C. W. Wahl, "The Relation Between Primary and Secondary Identifications," in Eugene Burdick and Arthur J. Brodbeck, *American Voting Behavior,* pp. 262–80.

27. Sebastian DeGrazia, "A Note on the Psychological Position of the Chief Executive," *Psychiatry,* 8 (1945), 267–72; W. R. D. Fairbairn, *An Object Relations Theory of Personality* (New York, Basic Books, 1954), pp. 223–29; Franz Alexander, "Emotional Factors in Voting Behavior," in Burdick and Brodbeck, *American Voting Behavior,* pp. 300–07; Richard E. Renneker, "Some Psychodynamic Aspects of Voting Behavior," ibid., pp. 399–413.

28. Harold Orlansky, "Reactions to the Death of President Roosevelt," *Journal of Social Psychology,* 26 (1947), 235–66, esp. 243. Also see Bernard Asbell, *When FDR Died* (New York, Holt, Rinehart and Winston, 1961).

He was just like a daddy to me always; he always talked to
me just that way. (Democratic Representative Lyndon Johnson of Texas.)

He was father and brother to us all. (Frank Sullivan.)

The death of Edward VII of England was the occasion for the
following piece of popular doggerel:

Greatest sorrow England ever had
When death took away our dear Dad.[29]

The massive public response to the assassination of President
John F. Kennedy in 1963 brought forth a variety of research
reports confirming the impression that intensively felt attachments
with figures in the remote environment, especially the president,
are prevalent even though the presence of such attachments is
not ordinarily apparent. There is a good bit of evidence that children as well as adults were emotionally affected by Kennedy's
death. And at least in some specialized populations of children,
namely children undergoing psychotherapy, feelings toward
family members were very much implicated in responses to the
President's death.[30]

For adults, as Sheatsley and Feldman comment, it was "difficult
to picture the youthful, fun-loving Kennedys as serving *in loco
parentis.*"[31] Nevertheless, statements such as the following (which
were made by college students shortly after the assassination)[32]

29. Kingsley Martin, *The Magic of Monarchy* (New York, Knopf, 1937),
p. 19.

30. Numerous studies of public reaction to President Kennedy's assassination are reported in Greenberg and Parker, eds., *Communication in Crisis.* On
the reactions of children in therapy see the papers by Augusta Alpert, Martha
Wolfenstein, Joan J. Zilbach, Gilbert Kliman, and Othilda Krug in a forthcoming volume to be edited by Martha Wolfenstein and Gilbert Kliman.

31. Paul B. Sheatsley and Jacob J. Feldman, "The Assassination of President
Kennedy: A Preliminary Report on Public Reactions and Behavior," *Public
Opinion Quarterly, 28* (1964), pp. 189–215.

32. Greenstein, "College Student Reactions to the Assassination of President
Kennedy."

suggest that the magnitude of grief was as great, if not quite as enduring, as would be expected in the death of a member of the immediate family, or a very close friend.

Well, a friend of mine [died in an accident] several years ago. We had a room near each other in the [dormitory] that year and we were real good buddies, and when he died I found out about it sort of matter of factly—somebody assumed that I already knew—and I felt sort of guilty that one of my reactions was that, well, X's gone, you know. And, in a way it was, how could he do that to me? How could he leave me? In the loss you felt that there was a personal anger . . . and this is very similar to what I felt about Kennedy, and yet with Kennedy it was not only me, but the whole country. It was not so much that Kennedy was dead, but that I was without a friend and a leader, and so was the whole country. It had become sort of queer. Well, my mother's been in the hospital recently, you know, and kind of ill. In a kind of a way I felt that it would be better if she had died rather than Kennedy.

I had a cousin who died of sleeping sickness about three years ago, who I didn't know too well, and I didn't give a damn, actually. And I felt more strongly about this, and God knows I knew her better. I didn't know Kennedy at all —I've never met the man. I did feel some sort of identification, and I can't say why because I wasn't a rabid Kennedyite.

The only experience I've had with death is that my grandfather died after two years of the state that Joseph Kennedy is in now and it wasn't pleasant. And at the time I vividly recall that I was sorry, but not upset like this, like I was Friday. . . . Somehow I felt when I heard this news like I think I might have felt if I'd been told someone real close to me had died. It's something I can't . . . I've tried to explain to myself and I can't.

The existing fragments of quantitative evidence are ambiguous on the hypothesis that citizens unconsciously link primary and secondary environment figures and respond to the latter in terms of the former. However, verification is made difficult (although not, as has been alleged, impossible) by the evident complexity of such a process and the variable forms it might take. A public figure (for example, President Kennedy) might take on the characteristics of a family member without specifically serving as a parent surrogate; he might serve as a sibling, a son, even as a composite of several family members. Furthermore, for some people, the unconscious linkage of immediate and secondary environment figures may be a simple generalization from the former to the latter, but for others there may be more devious compensatory associations. Thus, for example, for one individual, hostility toward primary group figures such as the father may lead to hostility to other authority figures such as the president. For another individual, primary group hostilities may be reacted to by idealizing public figures.[33] Research on the psychoanalytic hypo-

33. Judith V. Torney, in an analysis of portions of the data collected by Easton and Hess, reports findings consistent with (but not directly demonstrative of) the hypothesis that idealization of political authority is compensatory —that it forms in reaction to unsatisfactory experiences with paternal authority. "The Child's Idealization of Authority" (unpublished M.A. thesis, University of Chicago Library, 1962). She suggests a possible connection with George R. Bach's findings on "Father-Fantasies and Father-Typing in Father-Separated Children," *Child Development*, 17 (1946), 63–80. Possible reaction-formation relationships between authority experiences in the family and responses to nonfamily authority are suggested in Leroy S. Burwen, "A Study of Attitudes toward Authority" (unpublished Ph.D. dissertation, University of Chicago Library, 1954), and Leroy S. Burwen and Donald T. Campbell, "The Generality of Attitudes toward Authority and Nonauthority Figures," *Journal of Abnormal and Social Psychology*, 54 (1957), 24–31. John E. Teahan and Sanford Golin, on the other hand, found what seemed to be a direct generalization of attitudes in a study of reactions to President Kennedy's assassination. Among male (but not female) college students the tendency to respond impersonally to the President's death was greater if the individual's feelings toward his father or brother were negative. "Reaction to the Death of the President as a Function of Sex, Ideology, Symbolic Significance and Perception of Family Figures," mimeographed, 1964. Also relevant are Benson H. Marsten and James C. Coleman, "Specificity of Attitudes toward Paternal and Non-Paternal Authority

theses about authority therefore will require considerable ingenuity of conceptualization and technique. In particular, it will be important to specify and measure the conditions under which one or another type of linkage between primary and secondary environment figures takes place.[34] For the present purposes, we may simply note that one source of the imagery of benevolence, protectiveness, and extreme sagacity in children's descriptions of leaders *could* prove to be unconscious processes of the sort suggested in psychoanalytic theory.

As we have seen, the child's glowing political imagery shows signs of attrition (mainly in the use of "benevolent" language)

Figures," *Journal of Individual Psychology, 17* (1961), 96–101; Robert A. LeVine, "The Role of the Family in Authority Systems: A Cross-Cultural Application of Stimulus-Generalization Theory," *Behavioral Science, 5* (1960), 291–96 and "The Internalization of Political Values in Stateless Societies," *Human Organization, 19* (1960), 51–58; Aron Wolfe Siegman, "An Empirical Investigation of the Psychoanalytic Theory of Religious Behavior," *Journal for the Scientific Study of Religion, 1* (1961), 75–78; Ross Stagner, "Attitude toward Authority: An Exploratory Study," *Journal of Social Psychology, 40* (1954), 197–210. For an attempt to explain the idealization of political leaders by young children largely in terms of cognitive development and the child's increasingly realistic understanding of the punishments which can be administered by political leaders, see Lewis A. Froman, Jr., "Learning Political Attitudes," *Western Political Quarterly, 15* (1962), 304–13.

34. The hierarchical imagery reported in note 14 provides an illustration of one type of linkage which may take place. In each instance the child clearly has meager factual information about the roles he is attempting to describe. His allusion to a chain of command seems to result from an attempt to organize what fragmentary information he has. This may be seen in further detail in a follow-up interview with a sixth grade boy who had responded hierarchically on his questionnaire:

INTERVIEWER: What sorts of things does Mayor Lee do?

LARRY: Well, he keeps the city together and tells them what to do.

I: Tells who what to do?

L: Well, let's see. He probably tells some of the most important people and then they tell the ones that are less important and they keep on going.

I: What kinds of people are these? Do you mean *any* people in the city?

L: No, like the police chief and the head of the schools or something.

I: What do you think the governor does?

during preadolescence. The greatest change away from political euphoria probably is in adolescence. Disillusionment, following increased realistic political understanding, might produce such changes. Another likely cause would be the adolescent's need to assume adult mannerisms, including in some cases an inside dopester's appraisal of politics. Adolescence is, at any rate, a time for felling idols and perceiving the commanding figures of one's adult environment in a more fallible light.

Consequences of the child's view of political authority

How does knowledge that the political learning sequence is from childhood idealism to adult realism and cynicism add to our understanding of citizens' responses to political authority? To answer this some further remarks on adult orientations to political leaders are necessary.

The cynical imagery of Americans seems to have less effect on their political behavior than the positive side of their responses —their respect for high political leaders and roles, and their fre-

---

L: Well, he probably tells the mayors what to do and he probably tells other people what to do.

I: When you say "probably," does that mean you're sort of guessing about what he does?

L: Yes . . . He has to tell *somebody* what to do.

I: President Eisenhower, what does he do?

L: He probably tells the governors what to do.

I: Can you think of any other things that he might do?

L: He probably tells the people that are going to foreign countries to present a thing or something he wants that if they might be interested in.   [sic]

I: What kind of a thing do you mean?

L: Well, like a peace treaty or something.

That Larry turns "automatically" to hierarchy as an organizing principle suggests that his prepolitical experiences have taught him to view the world in terms of "telling people what to do." One might hypothesize, for example, that children responding in this way are more likely to come from families in which parental authority follows similar patterns.

quent willingness to hold individual leaders in great esteem. This is evident not merely from such relatively narrow phenomena as the increased esteem politicians receive once they are elected and the general willingness to accept the verdict of elections. Acceptance of, and even devotion to, authority is a pervasive phenomenon which we take for granted; it has an atmospheric ubiquity, ever-present yet inconspicuous. The oft-proclaimed stability of the American political system, in spite of a remarkably heterogeneous population, suggests that powerful psychological mechanisms encouraging political obedience are present in the citizenry. These mechanisms—along with, it should be added, the widespread disinterest of Americans in politics—may be as important as many of the more familiar historical, political, economic, and social factors that are drawn on to explain the complex phenomenon of political stability.

Favorable conceptions of political authority are an early acquisition. They emerge years before the child has more than a smattering of factual political information. Negative attitudes toward political leaders are chronologically late arrivals. Psychologists of various schools, ranging from psychoanalysis to learning theory, argue that "learning which takes place early in life should have especially great influence on lasting personality characteristics."[35] Similar conclusions have been reached by anthropologists, who hypothesize that the elements in a culture learned earliest in childhood are the elements most resistant to change.[36] It is possible, therefore, that when the adult is in conflict between his positive and negative assessments of political leaders, the longest held of these is most likely to influence his response. The hypothesis that early learning is especially potent learning also seems to fit other aspects of political development, both cognitive and affective. In

35. Child, "Socialization," p. 678.
36. Edward M. Bruner, "Cultural Transmission and Cultural Change," *Southwestern Journal of Anthropology, 12* (1956), 191–99; Melford Spiro, "The Acculturation of American Ethnic Groups," *American Anthropologist, 57* (1955), 1240–52. For further discussion of the significance of early learning see Chapter 4, pp. 79 ff.

Chapter 4 I shall develop more fully the argument that early learning is of fundamental importance.

"If," as Easton and Hess[37] note, "what is learned early in life is hard to displace in later years, we have here an important increment to our understanding of the sources of stability in the American political system." Early idealization of the president "should contribute to the ease with which members of the American political system develop a strong attachment to the structure of the regime." Moreover, "insofar as feelings generated with respect to the Presidency as a focal point are subsequently extended to include other parts of the political structure . . . this may well be the path through which members of the system come to value the whole structure."

37. Easton and Hess, "The Child's Political World."

The Development of Political Information
and Partisan Motivations

In the previous chapter we were concerned with an aspect of children's political orientations which remains relatively unchanged throughout the grade school years—the young child's rather idealized view of political authority. The main *developmental* change we noted in the child's view of authority was a slight shift during the fourth through eighth grade period away from idealization of leaders. Presumably if the sample had been extended to include adolescents and young adults a further development of considerable interest would have been evident—the advent of the cynicism toward politics which is so prevalent among adults.

Development is much more apparent during the grade school years when we shift attention from feelings toward leaders to *information about politics* and *partisan motivations*. Among fourth graders, political information scarcely goes beyond the vaguely positive dispositions toward the president and mayor discussed in Chapter 3. By eighth grade, children have become reasonably well informed about the major political institutions, if we take as our yardstick the level of political information of adults in the United States.[1] Partisan motivations also develop

1. As we shall see, the political awareness of older children *is* quite low by "ideal" standards. But so is the political awareness of adults in the United States (and, it seems, in the other democracies). For example, only 19 per cent of the adult electorate can name the three branches of government, a third can

during the grade school years, but the development of partisanship is more complex than the development of information.

I have suggested that the favorable feelings toward political
leaders acquired early in childhood seem to have a more substantial effect on the individual's adult political behavior than do the
various negative orientations toward politicians which emerge
later in life. A parallel observation can be made about the development of information and motivations. In general, *the more important a political orientation is in the behavior of adults, the
earlier it will be found to emerge in the learning of the child.*[2] To
support this generalization it will be necessary to consider literature on adult political behavior as well as the New Haven findings.

Throughout this chapter, findings are reported by socioeconomic
status (SES), distinguishing between children of white-collar and
blue-collar family backgrounds. Since part of my purpose is to
estimate basic norms of political development—i.e. ages at which
various patterns of information and motivation emerge—it is
helpful to deal with socially homogeneous groups. Doing so
compensates somewhat for the non-random nature of the sample
(the SES groups in the New Haven sample are not proportional
to their strength in the general population and many responses
vary by SES), so that the findings become more generalizable.

For convenience of exposition, the discussion focuses on developmental patterns in the upper SES subsample. The general
relationships I shall be dealing with also hold for lower SES
children—the latter simply tend to be less politically informed

---

identify the Bill of Rights, and about half know who is Secretary of State. See
Hazel Gaudet Erskine, "The Polls: Textbook Knowledge," *Public Opinion
Quarterly*, 27 (1963), 137–40. For a general discussion of voter information
see Fred I. Greenstein, *The American Party System and the American People*
(Englewood Cliffs, N.J., Prentice-Hall, 1963), pp. 12–16 and the references
there cited.

2. We cannot, however, reverse the order of this proposition and assert
that early political learning is *necessarily* influential in adult political behavior.
Some early learning (e.g. certain of the erroneous conceptions discussed in the
previous chapter, such as "the mayor pays working people like banks") is
unlearned and is not evident in adult political orientations. See p. 41 n. above.

and less politically involved at each age level. (Chapter 5 deals directly with political differences between upper and lower status children, at which point we shall return to a number of the tables presented here.)[3]

THE DEVELOPMENT OF POLITICAL INFORMATION

Table 4.1 traces the development of children's awareness of six major political institutions: the executives and legislatures at the local, state, and federal levels of government. We see the proportion of children who were able to describe with "reasonable accuracy" the functions of the mayor, governor, president, New Haven Board of Aldermen, Connecticut state legislature, and the Congress. We also see the proportion who were at least generally aware of the "public nature" of these institutions (i.e. the reasonably well-informed children, plus those with a vaguer understanding). And we see the proportion of children who could name the incumbent mayor, governor, and president. Here we have what might be considered a rough measure of whether an individual has the cognitive capacity for political participation, since an "ideal" citizen—one who used his vote effectively to reward and punish public servants—could be expected to have a rather clear conception of each of these six institutions.

3. Tests of significance of the socioeconomic status group differences are reported in the notes to each of the tables. I have used tests as a rule-of-thumb technique for deciding which findings to discuss in the analysis of class differences in Chapter 5 (and in the sex difference analysis in Chapter 6). It should be made clear, however, that the New Haven data are tentative and fall well short of the requirements of statistical inference. The "sample" was not random and, more important, the respondents are not independently selected. Of necessity the questionnaire was administered to *classrooms* of children and therefore findings can be seriously affected by the idiosyncrasies of each classroom—for example, by whether the teacher was attentive to social studies and current events, or whether she left these topics out of the curriculum. In the present chapter and in Chapter 3, I concentrate on discussing rather straightforward response distributions and developmental trends. I therefore have not reported levels of significance, or confidence intervals, since these would merely give a specious aura of reliability to the findings. The most appropriate test of the significance of all of the findings of the New Haven study is additional, replicative research. For further methodological points, see Appendix B.

TABLE 4.1. Children's Familiarity with Political Leaders and Institutions by School Year and Socioeconomic Status (SES)[a]

	Upper SES School Year				
	4	5	6	7	8
Mayor					
Reasonably accurate understanding of role	37%	45%	52%	76%	62%
Aware of public nature of role[b]	45	68	83	84	78
Knows name	92	95	98	100	100
Governor					
Reasonably accurate	8	16	35	37	49
Aware of public nature	20	38	61	60	62
Knows name	33	39	51	66	76
President					
Reasonably accurate	29	43	46	66	73
Aware of public nature	55	70	70	79	86
Knows name	96	100	96	100	100
Board of Aldermen					
Reasonably accurate	6	2	4	10	19
Aware of public nature	10	7	13	24	32
State Legislature					
Reasonably accurate	2	7	11	16	32
Aware of public nature	4	11	20	24	53
Congress					
Reasonably accurate	10	30	22	50	62
Aware of public nature	20	45	41	66	81
Total cases	49	56	46	38	37

a. In this and the following tables, SES differences were tested by chi square, using two-by-two contingency tables. Yates' correction for continuity was used in all computations. An overall combined probability for all five school years was determined for each row in the table by summation of the chi square values and degrees of freedom for the row. (For the technique of combining independent tests of significance, see R. A. Fisher, *Statistical Methods for Research Workers,* New York, Hafner, 1950, pp. 99–101.) None of the SES differences in the above table reach the five per cent level of significance. As has been noted, SES differences are discussed in Chapter 5 whereas the dis-

	Lower SES				
	School Year				
	4	5	6	7	8
Mayor					
Reasonably accurate understanding of role	31%	39%	49%	62%	68%
Aware of public nature of role[b]	39	58	83	84	84
Knows name	89	98	97[c]	99	96
Governor					
Reasonably accurate	8	8	19	36	42
Aware of public nature	19	18	38	52	59
Knows name	40	26	87[c]	66	73
President					
Reasonably accurate	19	24	49	65	65
Aware of public nature	34	50	71	77	84
Knows name	95	94	100	99	100[d]
Board of Aldermen					
Reasonably accurate	3	2	12	23	29
Aware of public nature	18	8	26	32	34
State Legislature					
Reasonably accurate	8	3	9	28	38
Aware of public nature	10	8	13	31	47
Congress					
Reasonably accurate	10	19	42	48	63
Aware of public nature	18	31	52	57	78
Total cases	62	62	69	97	143

cussion in this chapter is based mainly on developmental patterns in the upper SES subsample.

b. Sum of "reasonably accurate" responses and all other responses showing that a public role (or, in the case of legislatures, institution) is being described by the child.

c. Total cases in these cells 68, due to invalid responses.

d. Total cases in this cell 142, due to invalid response.

An overall impression of cognitive developing during the last five years of grade school may be had by glancing down the fourth through eighth grade columns of the portion of Table 4.1 reporting findings for the upper SES subsample. The modal fourth grader (i.e. the fourth grader whose response is shared by half of his age-mates) knows the names of the president and mayor and he also shows some general awareness of the "public nature" of the president's role. In each successive age group additional bits of information become evident:

Fifth graders show awareness of the mayor's role, as well as that of the president.

Sixth graders are the first group in which the modal child is familiar with the state level. At this age the governor's name is known and the public nature of his role is understood.

The seventh grade is the first at which children are able to characterize a legislature as well as an executive. At this point New Haven children were typically able to describe both of the major federal institutions, President and Congress.

In eighth grade, the fifth of the six institutions, the state legislature, is at least vaguely understood. Even in eighth grade few children can characterize the Board of Aldermen (although a majority claim to have heard of the city legislature).

Two aspects of this sequence of political learning can usefully be compared with what we know of adult political orientations—the order of learning about the three *levels of government* and about *executives and legislatures* at each governmental level.

Order of learning about levels of government

Children clearly are first aware of federal and local government; understanding of state government ordinarily does not come until sixth grade and even among sixth graders there is less awareness of who occupies the governorship than there is awareness of the incumbent president and mayor among fourth graders. The federal level is the first at which there is "full" understanding in the sense of awareness of both the executive (the president and his duties) and legislature (Congress).

Although there are no systematic survey data comparing adult information about the three levels of government, people have been asked which levels of government they consider most important. In one national survey, 51 per cent of the respondents ranked the federal government first among a series of institutions (such as large business organizations, labor unions, state governments) in terms of its "influence now on how things go in this country." A mere three per cent of this sample ranked state governments first. When asked which institutions *should* have the most influence, 62 per cent of the same respondents ranked the national government first; nine per cent ranked state government first.[4] Additional data, unfortunately from a survey of only one community, suggest that citizens consider both federal and local government more important than state government. When citizens of this community were asked which levels of government they considered "important" and "interesting" they made many fewer references to the state than to the other two governmental levels.[5]

Order of learning about executives and legislatures

At each level of government, awareness of the executive precedes awareness of the legislature. Understanding of executives also is much *richer* than understanding of legislatures: children make a greater number and a wider variety of statements in describing president than Congress, governor than state legislature, mayor than Board of Aldermen. Descriptions of legislatures tend

---

4. Harold Orlans, *Opinion Polls on National Leaders* (Philadelphia and Washington, Institute for Research in Human Relations, Report No. 6, 1953), pp. 2–12.

5. George Belknap and Ralph Smuckler, "Political Power Relations in a Mid-West City," *Public Opinion Quarterly*, 20 (1956), 80. These judgments were concurred in by both a sample of the community at large and a sample of the community's civic leaders.

to be pedantic and superficial, as in Judith's characterization of Congress: "I'm not too sure what it does. . . . About all the laws have to go through Congress, through different stages to become a law." Descriptions of executives show fewer of the earmarks of rote learning.

An added aspect of children's descriptions of legislative bodies is interesting because of the light it may shed on the effects of the learning *sequence.* A number of children volunteered the statement that the legislature at one or another level of government was subordinate to the executive. Congressmen and other legislators were described as the "helpers" of the president, governor, and mayor. In all, 60 such statements were spontaneously made about legislatures and only one of the 659 children described an executive as subordinate to a legislature.

Since the legislature normally is understood much later than the executive at the same level of government, it seems reasonable to hypothesize that something like the following cognitive process occurs: The child knows of the executive; he learns later that there are other officials associated with the executive; he assumes (more or less tacitly) that they must be the executive's assistants. Easton and Hess report a similar observation in Chicago. The president, they suggest, as the first major political figure of whom the children in their sample were aware,

> serves as a central orientation point for an increasing awareness of other elements of the political system. These other elements are initially seen in terms of their assumed relationship to the President himself. Thus [for example] . . . to the very young child . . . Congress is viewed as a group that takes orders from the President and performs certain tasks at his command.[6]

6. Robert D. Hess and David Easton, "The Child's Image of the President," *Public Opinion Quarterly,* 24 (1960), 634–35. Also see Fred I. Greenstein, "More on Children's Images of the President," *ibid.,* 25 (1961), 648–54. We may note that Chicago children, unlike New Haven children, evidently knew little about city officials. New Haven Mayor Lee's great activity (including, as

In the case of adults, there are no studies of whether president and Congress and the executives and legislatures at the other governmental levels are perceived in terms of superiority and subordination. But it is evident that adults are far better informed about executives than about legislatures. Awareness of the name of the incumbent president is almost universal: virtually no adult is unfamiliar with this primitive datum of American politics. Only about a third of national samples can name their congressman, or the senators from their state.[7] Indirect evidence suggests that at the state and local levels the gap between awareness of executive and legislators is as great, or greater.[8]

The foregoing is one basis for our generalization that the orientations which are most important in the political responses of adults are acquired earliest in childhood: executives are understood earlier than legislatures, and among adults there is greater awareness of the former than of the latter; federal and (in New Haven, at least) local government are understood before state government, and in the adult population state government is considered less important than federal or local government. We shall now consider the development of partisanship during the late grade school years.

---

we saw from Judith's comments, direct contacts with children) undoubtedly accounts for children's familiarity with him. In East Haven, a neighboring community, pre-test findings were that only 40 per cent of the fifth graders (in contrast to over 95 per cent of New Haven fifth graders) knew the city executive's name. On Mayor Lee see Robert A. Dahl, *Who Governs?* (New Haven, Yale University Press, 1961) and Raymond E. Wolfinger, *The Politics of Progress* (New Haven, Yale University Press, forthcoming).

7. Erskine, "The Polls: Textbook Knowledge"; Greenstein, *The American Party System and the American People.*

8. In particular, research on voting in nonpartisan jurisdictions supports this contention. Where party is not listed on the ballot, voters fluctuate from one election to the next in their support for incumbent executives, but they rarely vote incumbent legislators out of office. This suggests that familiarity with the activities of executives is substantial, but that little more is known than the names of incumbent legislators. For a fuller presentation of this argument and an indication of the relevant research see Greenstein, *The American Party System,* pp. 57–60.

THE DEVELOPMENT OF PARTISAN MOTIVATIONS

One classification of the factors motivating voters' election day choices that has proved useful in political research distinguishes between *candidate* orientation, *issue* orientation, and *party* identification. In other words, the voter's decision at the polls may constitute (1) a judgment of the merits of one or more of the candidates, (2) an assessment of the issues raised in the campaign, (3) a "standing choice," based on his attachment to a party, or (4) some combination of these.[9]

Each of these three classes of motivation has been shown to have an independent effect on voting. But of the three, party is by far the most influential in the United States. The Survey Research Center found in the 1952 election that when one controlled for whether a voter had favorable views of the Democratic and Republican candidates and whether he took the Democratic or Republican position on foreign and domestic policy, the partial correlation between party identification and presidential preference was .42. With similar controls, the other motivating factors were much less predictive of electoral choice: for example, the partial correlation between attitude toward Eisenhower and the disposition to vote for him was only .16, and the partial correlation between agreement with a party's stand on domestic policy and voting for the party was .23.[10]

As electoral research accumulates, it has become increasingly evident that voters' attachments to parties are crucially significant, not only for understanding individual voting behavior but also for explaining certain general characteristics of political systems. At the individual level, party identifications are ubiquitous and have a major effect on voting behavior. In the United States, a full 75 per cent of the adult population identifies with one or the other of the two major political parties. Attachment to a party

9. Campbell et al., *The Voter Decides.*

10. Angus Campbell and Donald Stokes, "Partisan Attitudes and the Presidential Vote," in Burdick and Brodbeck, eds., *American Voting Behavior,* pp. 356–57. Campbell, *The Voter Decides.*

is generally a lifelong commitment—only a few voters report that they ever have shifted party allegiance. There also is striking intergenerational continuity in party preferences—a minority of individuals depart from the party identifications held by their parents. Although in every election some party identifiers are sufficiently swayed by issues or candidates to vote for the opposing party's candidate, the preponderant tendency is to vote for one's own party. In fact, as of 1960 a full half of the American voting population reported that it had voted for the same party's candidates in *all* elections. The importance of party loyalties in accounting for this remarkable consistency of electoral behavior can be seen when we note that only five per cent of the people who classify themselves as independents have invariably voted for the same party.

The prevalence and stability of party identifications and their influence on electoral choice have a twofold significance for the political system. First, the distribution of party preferences in a given historical period will have a major effect on control of political office. In the United States, since 1932, there have been substantially more Democratic than Republican party identifiers. During this period the Republican party has controlled the presidency for only eight years and Congress for only four years. Secondly, the ability of existing parties to command the loyalty of the bulk of voters inhibits the rise of new political groupings. During the entire post-Civil War period, excepting the 1912 election, the two major American parties have commanded an overwhelming majority of the votes cast for national office.[11]

Just as the pervasive attachments of Americans to the Democratic and Republican parties help to explain the ability of the major parties to resist the encroachments of minor parties, there is no doubt that the persistence of the major parties in turn contributes to the prevalence of party identification and its strength as a determinant of voting. As a result of their long-term stability

11. For a further discussion of these assertions about party identification and the evidence on which they are based, see Greenstein, *The American Party System*, pp. 27–36.

and their monopoly of power, the Democratic and Republican parties are highly visible and therefore "available" as a basis of political choice. Candidates change over relatively short periods of time. So do specific issues. Sometimes a rather long series of elections will raise roughly the same ideological questions about, for example, the role of the federal government in economic activities and the nation's commitments in the international arena. However, only a small segment of the American electorate seems to have sufficiently articulated ideologies to make issue orientation a major determinant of the vote.[12] Typically, a voter will support a hodgepodge of "liberal" and "conservative" views on various issues rather than organizing his opinions on any consistent basis. The very terms "liberal" and "conservative" seem to be unfamiliar to much of the electorate.

It was not possible in the present study to parallel directly the indices used in surveys of adult candidate orientation, issue orientation, and party identification. Nevertheless, portions of our data shed light on the childhood roots of each motivational pattern.

The "immaturity" of children's candidate orientations

Our discussion, in Chapter 3, of children's feelings toward political leaders gives us some sense of their responses to candidates. Children were in no way reluctant to pass judgment on public officials. Very few failed to rate the president and the mayor (Table 3.2, p. 37); even the governor was evaluated by 70 per cent of the sample.

Nor is it surprising that children should be able to make some sort of an evaluative response to public figures. From an early age, beginning with the parents' characterization of the child himself as good or bad, and continuing, for example, through the distinctions made between good guys and bad guys in the entertainment media, the child learns to judge figures in both the remote and immediate environments. Yet, we also have seen that

12. Angus Campbell et al., *The American Voter* (New York, Wiley, 1960), pp. 216–65.

children seem more aware of the positive than of the negative aspects of public figures. They evidently are reluctant to evaluate leaders unfavorably. This suggests an "immature" pattern of candidate orientation: immature in the strictly statistical sense of being a pattern which is typical of childhood and disappears with increasing age, and evidently also in the sense of indicating an unformed critical capacity.

The late arrival of issue orientations

Issue or ideological orientation requires far more complex and demanding intellectual processes than candidate orientation. Pretest interviewing located one or two older children who showed a somewhat consistently liberal or conservative approach to politics. But it was far more common for children, at all age levels, merely to respond ad hoc with specific judgments about specific issues. Since among the younger age groups even this ability was absent —fourth, fifth, and sixth graders often were not sufficiently well informed to understand the sorts of statements which make up liberalism–conservatism scales—specific issue questions were not asked. We can, however, draw on responses to two open-ended questions, which, since it was possible to answer them in terms of issues, give us some sense of budding issue orientations.

Table 4.2 reports responses to the question, "Can you think of a difference between the Democrats and the Republicans?" and to "If you could change the world in any way you wanted, what change would you make?" The first of these questions was asked only of the upper three grades. The second, which was asked of the entire sample, was placed at the very end of the questionnaire, following a long series of items about politics and partisanship.

It is not until eighth grade that as many as half of the middle-class children offer *any* response to the question about party differences. Even then the responses often are close to tautological ("they are two sides"), or are vague references to differences in the personnel of the parties ("The Democrats and the Republicans put up different men"). References to issues increase from six to

TABLE 4.2. Children's References to "Ideology" and Political Issues by School Year and Socioeconomic Status[a]

	School Year				
Upper SES	4	5	6	7	8
Responds to party difference item[b]	—	—	23%	48%[c]	51%[d]
Refers to "issue" differences between the parties[b]	—	—	6	32[c]	42[d]
Refers to "ideological" differences between the parties[b]	—	—	2	8[c]	6[d]
Proposes political change	16%	44%	50	52	59
Total cases	49	56	46	38	37
Lower SES					
Responds to party difference item[b]	—	—	19%	23%	34%
Refers to "issue" differences between the parties[b]	—	—	6	5	20
Refers to "ideological" differences between the parties[b]	—	—	0	1	6
Proposes political change	3%	11%	42	39	52
Total cases	62	62	69	97	143

a. Reference to party differences, issue differences, and political change differ significantly by SES ($p < .01$).

b. The item was, "Can you think of a difference between the Democrats and the Republicans?" Row one reports the proportion of respondents able to make any statement other than "don't know." Row two reports all references to issues among the various responses, and row three reports specifically "ideological" issue references. Item not administered to fourth and fifth graders.

c. Total cases 37; item not administered to one child.

d. Total cases 36; item not administered to one child.

42 per cent between sixth and eighth grades. But most of the issue references are vague (for example, the statement that the two parties "think differently") and unrelated to the broader ideological questions that tend to divide the national leadership of the two parties. Analyzing the responses in terms of the Survey Research Center's index of ideological sophistication,[13] we find that only six per cent of the eighth graders make the kinds of state-

13. Ibid., pp. 216 f.

ments made by the "most sophisticated" 51 per cent of the adult population—references to a generalized liberal–conservative ideology and references to social class and other group differences in the party constituencies. These are the rare children who make statements such as:

> When the Republicans win some men get out of work.

> One [party] is mostly on the business side of things, the Republicans.

> The Republicans are for the rich people.

> The Democrats are too free with money.

The question about "changes in the world" admits of an almost endless range of possible answers. As we see in Table 4.2, references to political changes are increasingly common among older children. Fourth graders frequently used the item as a springboard for some distinctly juvenile fantasy: "I would make all of the candy in all of the candy stores free." By sixth grade a majority of the responses were political. The political statements were rarely partisan, much less ideological; most common by far (perhaps stimulated by recent summit conferences) was simply the wish for peace. However, it seems likely that this developmental pattern should give us some insight into the growth of the *capacity* for holding issue or ideological orientations.

In the middle-class subsample there is a striking increase in political wishes between fourth and fifth grade (ages nine and ten). This roughly parallels the point at which various observers of child behavior have seen a more general decrease in childhood egocentrism, preoccupation with the immediate environment, and inability to think in abstract terms.

To Gesell and Ilg (who also base their observations on a sample of middle-class New Haven children) the ten-year-old is a substantially different individual from the nine-year-old. "He is so adaptively and diversely in touch with the adult environment that he seems . . . to be an adult in the making." Nine-year-old children, they find, tend typically to be intensely preoccupied with mastering various "visual, manual, and laryngeal skills."

> [The nine-year-old] works with channelized intentness and is not too easily diverted from one activity to another. He is in a more or less constant state of urgency, as though in contest with time. In comparison . . . [the ten-year-old] is relaxed and casual, yet alert. He has himself and his skills in hand. . . . Since his whole organization is less channelized his attitudes are more flexible, and he is more responsive to slight cues.

They go on to suggest:

> This relative fluidity has important cultural implications. It makes the ten-year-old peculiarly receptive to social information, to broadening ideas and to prejudices, good and bad. It is relatively easy to appeal to his reason. He is ready to participate in elementary discussions of social problems.[14]

Piaget and his associates also find at approximately this age a shift in children's intellectual development—away from the concrete and toward the stage at which "formal, abstract thought operations" are possible.[15]

It is at best speculative to suggest a connection between these observations of Gesell and Ilg and of Piaget and the development of issue orientation in New Haven children. But if there is a connection, an interesting hypothesis suggests itself. There may be a psycho-physiological stage before which it simply is not possible for children to acquire one class of adult orientation—the generalized ideological disposition. To paraphrase the jargon of

14. Arnold Gesell and Francis L. Ilg, *The Child from Five to Ten* (New York, Harper, 1946), pp. 636–37.

15. See, for example, Barbel Inhelder, "Some Aspects of Piaget's Genetic Approach to Cognition," in *Thought of the Child,* ed. William Kessen and Clementina Kuhlman (Yellow Springs, Ohio, Society for Research in Child Development, 1962), pp. 27–28. For a useful summary discussion of Piaget's work see John H. Flavell, *The Developmental Psychology of Jean Piaget* (Princeton, Van Nostrand, 1963).

educational psychology, it may be necessary for the child to reach a stage of ideology-readiness, before he can become, in the generic sense of the terms,

> either a little Liber*al*
> or else a little Conservat*iv*e.

As we shall see, no such barrier impedes the acquisition of party identifications.

The early development of party identifications

We have already seen that children's issue orientations are so underdeveloped that by eighth grade only about four tenths of the middle-class children could describe issue difference between the parties and only slightly more than half could describe any differences at all. We might therefore suspect that party identification is uncommon among children.

Table 4.3 shows how definitely this is *not* the case. By fourth grade more than six out of ten of the New Haven children were able to state whether their party preference was Republican or Democratic: this although little more than a third of the fourth graders could name even one public representative from either of the two major parties and less than a fifth could name a leader of each of the parties.[16] The prevalence of party identifications

16. Two items were used to elicit the statements about party leaders: "Who do you think is the most famous Republican?" "Who do you think is the most famous Democrat?" The level of response may have been somewhat lowered by the phrase "most famous," since some children who could identify a party leader may have had doubts about his fame. Follow-up interviewing suggested that the item wording did not have this effect. In no case was a child able to name a party leader if he had failed to respond to the relevant item. In general, paper-and-pencil questionnaires tend to underestimate respondents' information and shorten responses. However, the follow-up interviews suggested that the paper-and-pencil technique did not introduce serious distortions. For example, in no follow-up interview did a child respond to any of the items he had failed to respond to in the written instrument. (Below fourth grade writing difficulties *do* cut down sharply on responses, especially to open-ended items.) In the age groups studied here, the major effect of the paper-and-pencil technique is to reduce richness of responses and, of course, to make probes impossible. Cf. Appendix B.

among nine-year-olds is especially striking when we realize that
the proportion of adult Americans who identify with parties (75
per cent) is not much greater. In fact, in the 21–24-year-old segment of the adult population the frequency of party identification is identical to that of New Haven fourth graders.[17]

Here, as in children's assessments of the importance of political
roles, we find that political feelings, evaluations, and attachments
form well before the child learns the relevant supporting information. It is not until fifth grade that the modal child can name at
least one party leader, and not until eighth grade that children
typically name leaders of both parties.

The prevalence of party identifications among New Haven
children cannot be attributed to "response errors," such as guessing, or the arbitrary checking of alternatives on the questionnaire.
Children's party preferences correlate appropriately with the
demographic patterns of partisanship in New Haven. They also
are positively associated with favorable evaluations of leaders of
the same parties.

The source of these preferences is, as often has been noted in
the voting literature, the family. Only a handful of children in
the entire sample indicated that their own party preferences dif-
fered from those of their parents. In interviews children explicitly

17. The frequency of party identification in the adult population is reported
in various of the Survey Research Center studies; for example, *The Voter
Decides.* I am indebted to Angus Campbell for informing me of the frequency
of party identification among young voters. For a tabulation of party identification by age, which does not include the small proportion of the electorate
classified as "apolitical" and which therefore indicates a somewhat larger
proportion of identifiers, especially in the younger age groups, see *The American Voter,* p. 162. The rather low frequency of party attachments among upper
SES eighth graders probably results from an idiosyncracy of the sample. This
cell contains the smallest number of cases in the sample, and among lower SES
eighth graders there is no comparable decline in party identification. For evidence that both in the general population and in a specialized population of
children attending church schools party identification reaches a stable level by
eighth grade, see Daniel R. Leatherman, "The Political Socialization of Students
in the Mennonite Secondary Schools," *The Mennonite Quarterly Review,* 36
(1962), 90.

TABLE 4.3. Children's Orientations toward Partisan Politics by School Year and Socioeconomic Status (SES)[a]

| | School Year | | | | |
	4	5	6	7	8
Upper SES					
Has a party preference	63%	66%	61%	71%	49%
Calls self independent (written in)	2	5	4	13	16
Names leaders of both parties	18	27	33	47	59
Total naming party leaders[b]	38	61	66	65	75
Total cases	49	56	46	38	37
Lower SES					
Has a party preference	63%	56%	56%	67%	61%
Calls self independent (written in)	0	0	3	2	3
Names leaders of both parties	14	18	25	31	36
Total naming party leaders[b]	35	39	42	51	60
Total cases	62	62	69	97	143

a. The following SES differences are significant: calls self independent ($p < .02$); total naming party leaders ($p < .02$). SES differences in "names leader of both parties" approach significance ($p < .10$).

b. Includes children naming leaders of both parties and children naming only one party leader.

speak of party as an attribute of the family. (Judith says, "All I know is *we're* not Republicans.")[18] Party identifications probably develop without much explicit teaching on the part of parents, more or less in the form of a gradual awareness by the child of something which is part of him. The process doubtless is similar to the development of ethnic and religious identifications.

That party identifications are so common among young New Haven children lends support to Hyman's assertion that "the

18. Herbert Hyman has summarized the evidence on family transmission of party preference, most of which is based upon adults' reports of their parents' party identifications and of their own. Hyman points out that it is not fully clear whether this evidence demonstrates learning in the family or simply is "the *expected value* of correlations between pairs of *unrelated* individuals, who might be in the same social stratum, place of residence, etc." *Political Socialization,* p. 72. A number of aspects of the New Haven data

adult pattern that seems established in most complete form in earlier life is that of party affiliation."[19] More specifically, it seems to be the *direction* of party affiliation which is set early in life. We have already seen that it is some years until the party preference becomes grounded in such elementary information as whether the president is a Republican or a Democrat. We may also assume that children's party identifications are not as *intense* as they will be in later years, since even in adult life party attachments become stronger with age.[20]

I have suggested that a general factor in children's cognitive development—the inability of young children to think in abstract terms—may impede the formation of issue orientations. A fundamental psychological process, identification, may be at work to assist the formation of party loyalty. Although the process of identification is not well understood, and knowledge is especially sparse about secondary identifications (such as those with religious denomination, ethnic group, and party), identifications seem to be a vital part of the individual's development. They make it possible for him to both relate himself to, and distinguish himself from, others. Therefore one element in the earliness of party identifications, and in their subsequent stability, may be that they help maintain a sense of personal identity, as well as a link between the child, his parents, and other significant individuals and groups.[21]

---

strongly suggest that the family *is* the agent of transmission: viz., the direct statements of a number of children in the interviews (e.g. Judith); children's reported agreement with their parents (which is a good bit higher than their report of agreement with friends); and children's statements, in response to one of the questionnaire items, that they would turn to their parents (in lieu of friends, neighbors, teachers, etc.) as sources of voting information. Cf. the discussion of politics in the child's immediate circle in Fred I. Greenstein, "Children's Political Perspectives: A Study of the Development of Political Awareness and Preferences in Pre-Adolescents" (unpublished Ph.D. dissertation, Yale University Library, 1959), pp. 224–32.

19. *Political Socialization*, p. 46.

20. Campbell, *The American Voter*, pp. 161–67.

21. For indications of the state of the literature on identification see, for example: Robert P. Knight, "Introjection, Projection and Identification,"

That identifications form easily and serve valuable functions for the individual does not, it should be added, provide us with an exhaustive explanation of why party identifications are so stable. We have already (p. 66) noted how the continuity of the two major American parties and their monopoly of power makes them available as objects of identification. Stability of party identification doubtless is fostered also by the flexibility of the parties on matters of ideology, which makes them hospitable to a heterogeneous membership; by the tendency of members of the same social class and ethnic group to have the same party attachments and therefore (since social relations are most often with members of the same group) to associate mainly with like-minded partisans; and by the low saliency of politics to Americans, which makes party an unlikely area for adolescent rebellion.[22]

In the area of partisan motivation, then, as with the development of information, the importance of an orientation in adult political behavior is presaged by early childhood learning. Party preferences form before issue orientation, and before "mature" candidate orientation takes place. We may now consider some of the reasons for and results of the various sequences of development discussed in this chapter.

CAUSES AND CONSEQUENCES OF THE SEQUENCE OF DEVELOPMENT

Causes of the sequence of development

One obvious reason why children learn first about the institutions which are best understood and considered most important

---

Psychoanalytic Quarterly, 9 (1940), 334–41; Nevitt Sanford, "The Dynamics of Identification," *Psychological Review*, 62 (1955), 106–18; L. M. Lazowick, "On the Nature of Identification," *Journal of Abnormal and Social Psychology*, 51 (1955), 175–83; Jerome Kagan, "The Concept of Identification," *Psychological Review*, 65 (1958), 296–305; Daniel Glaser, "Dynamics of Ethnic Identification," *American Sociological Review*, 23 (1958), 31–40.

22. See Russell Middleton and Snell Putney, "Political Expression of Adolescent Rebellion," *American Journal of Sociology*, 68 (1963), 527–35 and the sources there cited.

by American adults is that these are the institutions adults are likely to discuss in the presence of children and to be able to explain and answer questions about. Both adults and children are in the same net of communications which constitutes the American political culture. One aspect of this culture is that the different political institutions and roles vary in status and recognition. Politicians themselves, although they give lip service to the formally coordinate status of president and Congress, of state and federal governments, do not esteem the various governmental institutions equally. Congressmen normally meet with the president in the White House, not on Capitol Hill. On the rare occasions when the president does come to Capitol Hill it is to address the Congress collectively and present it with *his* conception of the state of the union and of what the Congressional agenda should be. Congressionally minded politicians such as Robert A. Taft often have shown their readiness to seek the nomination for president, but no president has resigned from office to run for Congress, or for state office.

In the mass media—which shape and reinforce adult political values and also are a prime source of children's political learning —attention to the presidency exceeds attention to Congress.[23] New Haven's Mayor Lee, at the time of this study, rarely was absent from the front pages of the local press (in addition to appearing weekly on television, and frequently in person throughout the city). The Board of Aldermen, which then was little more than a ratifier of decisions by the city administration, meets weekly, and then sometimes is reported only on the inside pages of the newspaper. State political coverage is spotty in New Haven, especially coverage of the legislature, which meets biennially for a five-month session.

What children are exposed to also may help explain the earlier acquisition of party identification than of issue orientation. The parties are mentioned with at least moderate frequency in the child's face-to-face environment and in the media. Specific

23. Elmer Cornwell, Jr., "Presidential News: The Expanding Public Image," *Journalism Quarterly, 36* (1959), 275–85.

issues are presented largely during the brief period of the election campaign (and then the dominant impression probably is of the candidates themselves and not their utterances); broad ideologies are rarely presented at all, especially in the child's face-to-face environment, since these are of little significance to the adult population.

Such environmental influences are reinforced by children's own predispositions: what they are able to learn and interested in learning. It often has been pointed out that single executives are more easily dramatized, perceived, and understood than are such complex institutions as legislative assemblies. As Bagehot commented, almost a century ago, of the English monarchy, "the action of a single will, the fiat of a single mind, are easy ideas: anybody can make them out, and no one can ever forget them."[24] It is relatively simple to become aware of individual executives; legislators are easily lost in the crowd of their colleagues, and the legislative process is complex and difficult to follow.

Similarly, the parties are simple perceptual objects. They are stable, there are only two of them, and children often are aware of their personified symbols, the donkey and the elephant. Furthermore children readily form identifications at an early age. In contrast, issue orientation does not form easily or simply. As we noted in connection with the relative lack of importance of issues in adult voting behavior, specific issues change from campaign to campaign and the sheer number of political issues is bewildering. While ideology provides a convenient basis for organizing and simplifying the chaos of issues, few children are exposed to ideologies, and young children probably are unable to engage in the abstract cognitive operations inherent in ideological thinking. It is interesting to note that in France, where the parties are vastly more varied than in the United States, and where the complexities and ideological nuances of partisanship puzzle and frustrate a large

24. Walter Bagehot, *The English Constitution* (London, Oxford University Press, 1928, first published 1867), p. 30. Bagehot's point, of course, was that *adults* find it simple to perceive a single official; for children this would be even more the case.

part of the adult population, far fewer children acquire party identifications from their parents.[25]

Consequences of the sequence of development

My argument so far can be briefly summarized: the political orientations which are most important in the behavior of adults arise earliest in the childhood learning sequence; this is so partly because these are the orientations adults are most likely to display before children; but the sequence of learning is also affected by what children are able to absorb at various ages. We may now consider whether the sequence of learning has consequences. Does it make any difference that executives are understood before legislatures; federal, and probably also local, government before state government; party loyalty before issue orientation?

The importance of the learning sequence, and particularly of early learning, is asserted not only in contemporary psychological theory, but also in a good bit of our traditional common-sense lore. To understand the mature man, Tocqueville comments,

> we must see the first images which the external world casts upon the dark mirror of his mind, the first occurrences that

25. Philip E. Converse and Georges Dupeux, "Politicization of the Electorate in France and the United States," *Public Opinion Quarterly*, 26 (1962), 1–23. This extraordinarily interesting article shows, inter alia, that French voters are extremely puzzled by the complexities of their party system, that relatively few of them (less than 45 per cent) identify with parties, and that it is quite uncommon for French voters to have any knowledge of what their parents' party preferences were. (Only 28 per cent of a national sample could characterize their father's party preference, in contrast to 82 per cent in the United States.) The authors do not speculate on the causes of the failure of the French family to transmit party preference. This seems only in part to be a consequence of the infrequency of party preferences. One element may be the controversial nature of politics in France. Another may be related to French family structure; the role of the child seems to be much more compartmentalized and set off from adults than in the United States. Cf. Laurence Wylie, *Village in the Vaucluse* (Cambridge, Harvard University Press, 1951), especially Chapters 3–5. This work is generally interesting for what it suggests about the relationships between socialization practices and adult behavior, political and otherwise.

he witnesses; we must hear the first words which awaken the sleeping powers of thought, and stand by his earliest efforts if we would understand the prejudices, the habits, and the passions which will rule his life.[26]

Unfortunately, even though the problem is a classic one, there has been little systematic attention to the relative impact of early and late learning on adult behavior. Most of the research on early learning has been addressed to a quite restricted range of infant care practices, and even these have not been related to later behavior in a fully satisfactory fashion.[27] There also has been a good bit of attention to short-run learning sequences in adult life, studies of the effect of the order of presentation in persuasion.[28] But the sequence of social (including political) learning, especially during preadolescence, has not been examined.

The age at which learning takes place and the phasing of learning seem to be important in two ways: early learning takes place *during a formative period* and early learning *affects later learning*.

THE FORMATIVE NATURE OF EARLY LEARNING. The preschool years and the early school years are a time of great plasticity and receptivity: nothing in later life can compare with this period for the sheer volume of learning that takes place. The most commonly accepted assumptions of a culture—for example, assumptions about the structure of the family and kinship—are typically acquired during this period. And there is evidence that the culture

26. Alexis de Tocqueville, *Democracy in America, 1* (New York, Knopf, Vintage Books), 27–28.

27. One of the better known critiques of this literature is Harold Orlansky, "Infant Care and Personality," *Psychological Bulletin,* 47 (1949), 1–48. For a rejoinder to Orlansky and an extended bibliography see Sidney Axelrad, "Infant Care and Personality Reconsidered; Rejoinder to Orlansky," in *The Psychoanalytic Study of Society,* ed. Warner Muensterberger and Sidney Axelrad (New York, International Universities Press, 1962), 2, 75–132.

28. See the summary of literature on the effects of primacy and recency on learning in Carl I. Hovland et al., *Communication and Persuasion* (New Haven, Yale University Press, 1953), pp. 121–30, and Carl I. Hovland et al., *The Order of Presentation in Persuasion* (New Haven, Yale University Press, 1957).

content which is taught first to young children is least likely to change in the face of contact with other cultures. For example, Bruner finds that the aspects of the culture of the Mandan-Hidatsa Indians of North Dakota which traditionally were learned late in life have now vanished. "That which persists" among the contemporary Mandan-Hidatsa, "i.e. kinship, role conceptions, and values, was learned early, and the primary agents of cultural transmission were members of ego's lineage" (as opposed to more distant relatives and non-kin).[29] Spiro, in an analysis of the acculturation of American ethnic groups, finds similar evidence for the persistence of early learning: for example, eating habits, which are among "the first to be socialized," have commonly persisted long after other ethnic ways are abandoned. "This," he comments, "is what might be termed the 'onion-peel' nature of acculturation—the layers which are formed first are the ones to be peeled last."[30]

There are a number of reasons why we would expect this to be the case. First, the immature child is likely to learn uncritically: he is not conscious of alternatives and he lacks standards for judging information. Secondly, much of early learning takes place at a nonconscious level, through processes such as imitation and identification. What we learn without being conscious that we *are* learning is likely to be accepted as a given—a "fact of nature."[31]

29. Edward M. Bruner, "Cultural Transmission and Cultural Change," *Southwestern Journal of Anthropology, 12* (1956), 191–99.

30. Melford Spiro, "The Acculturation of American Ethnic Groups," *American Anthropologist, 57* (1955), 1240–52. For a summary of literature on the long-term persistence in a language of the vocabulary learned early in childhood see D. H. Hymes, "Lexicostatistics So Far," *Current Anthropology, 1* (1960), 5. For a general discussion of the political significance of early learning see Robert A. LeVine, "Political Socialization and Culture Change," in *Old Societies and New States,* ed. Clifford Geertz (New York, The Free Press of Glencoe, 1963), pp. 280–303.

31. This seems to be what Plato had in mind in the portion of his royal lie in which citizens, after having been instructed extensively in the appropriate virtues and duties for their station in the polity, "are to be told that their youth was a dream, and the education and training which they received . . . an appearance only; in reality during all that time they were being formed and

In addition, as Bruner notes, the agents of the young child's learning—his parents—are highly authoritative. Finally, early learning takes place at a time when fundamental personality characteristics are being formed. Social and political learning which takes place at this point can become a part of the individual's basic psychic equipment. (As I have suggested, a case in point may be party identification.)

For all of these reasons, it would not be surprising if the age at which learning takes place, *in and of itself,* were significant in explaining the later importance of orientations which are learned early. In other words, it is possible not only that children learn first of executives and of federal and local government because adults take these institutions most seriously, but also that adults are attentive to these institutions, in part, because these were the first about which they learned. In effect, the socialization process would serve, circularly, to reinforce the status quo.

EFFECTS OF EARLY LEARNING ON LATER LEARNING. Even if early learning were not independently significant, it would be important because it begins the learning sequence. As Irvin Child points out, "tendencies first acquired can shape later learning."[32] Learning invariably is selective and early learning can determine which segments of reality are selected and incorporated into the individual's frame of reference at later stages of his development. "Once a concept develops," O. J. Harvey and his associates comment, "it serves as an experiential filter through which impinging

fed in the womb of the earth, where they themselves and their arms and appurtenances were manufactured; when they were completed, the earth, their mother sent them up; and so, their country being their mother and also their nurse, they are bound to advise for her good, and to defend her against attacks, and her citizens they are to regard as children of the earth and their own brothers." *The Republic,* iii. I am indebted to Roger Masters for pointing out the significance of this passage to me. For a discussion of the program of political education in *The Republic* translated into contemporary psychological terms see Harold D. Lasswell, "Political Constitution and Character," *Psychoanalysis and the Psychoanalytic Review,* 46 (1960), 1–18.

32. Irvin Child, "Socialization," *Handbook of Social Psychology,* 2, 678–79.

82   *Children and Politics*

events are screened, gauged, and evaluated, a process which determines in large part what responses can and will occur."[33]

Thus I have suggested that it is because the child first learns of the executive and only later becomes aware of the legislature that he slips into thinking of the lawmaking body as inferior.[34] A further finding of the New Haven study, which also illustrates the possible ways in which early learning can affect later learning, was the tendency of a number of children to describe the governor—and even the president—in terms of an activity for which the incumbent mayor had received great publicity, urban redevelopment. Numerous children described Mayor Lee as a man who "cleans up the city's slums"; some also described the other executives in this fashion, obviously extrapolating from the one public figure whose image was clear and readily understood in order to explain the additional, more dimly perceived public officials.

The likelihood that early learning will have a vital effect on later learning seems to be especially great in the case of partisan motivations. Party identification, learned as it is uncritically and at an early age, can readily become "an experiential filter." It has been well documented that adult party identifiers evaluate new political developments in terms of their party preference, and that they may even selectively perceive the information most favorable to their own party position.[35] In early childhood, party

33. O. J. Harvey et al., *Conceptual Systems and Personality Organization* (New York, Wiley, 1961), pp. 2–3. Also see Phyllis A. Katz, "Effect of Labels on Children's Perception and Discrimination Learning," *Journal of Experimental Psychology, 66* (1963), 423–28.

34. Although legislatures are formally coordinate with executives in constitutional theory, there certainly is a good bit of accuracy in the perception that today they are subordinate to the executive. Thus descriptions of Congress as "the President's helpers" in fact are rather realistic. However, I doubt that children's assertions of this are in any important way based upon realistic perception of the status of contemporary legislatures. Their information about legislatures—from formal instruction or other sources—is far too skimpy for this to be so.

35. See, for example, Campbell, *The American Voter*, pp. 120–45, especially p. 135. Also Bernard Berelson et al., *Voting* (Chicago, University of Chicago Press, 1954), pp. 215–33.

preferences undoubtedly are an imperfect filter, since the child has not added to his identification the minimum degree of supporting information necessary to use it: for example, knowledge of who the public representatives of his party are. At this age, children probably acquire party-related beliefs (such as candidate evaluations) directly from their parents. By eighth grade, however, most children can identify the party leaders, and therefore are capable of using their party preferences as tools of choice. The utility of party identifications as cognitive tools may, in fact, be an additional cause of their strength and persistence.

CONSEQUENCES FOR THE POLITICAL SYSTEM. "The early family socialization process," Almond has commented, "is . . . one of the most important factors making for the resistance to social and political change."[36] The New Haven findings on the sequence of children's political development serve as something of a gloss on this assertion, for we have seen that early political learning seems to maintain, perhaps even reinforce, adult political priorities. This tendency of socialization processes to support the status quo also will be evident in the analyses which follow, in Chapters 5 and 6, of social class and sex differences in children's political development.

Some aspects of the political learning sequence undoubtedly have little effect on the individual's adult behavior and therefore are of no particular significance for the political system. For example, it is not likely that the perception by New Haven children of the governor or president in terms of the mayor has any lasting consequences. But assumptions that executives are superior to legislatures, or that federal officials are more important than state officials, *are* likely to persist, because they are consistent with beliefs already present in the political culture. These beliefs are relevant to the workings of the political system, since executives and legislatures and officials at various levels of government in

36. Gabriel A. Almond, "A Functional Approach to Comparative Politics," in Gabriel A. Almond and James S. Coleman, eds., *The Politics of Developing Areas* (Princeton, Princeton University Press, 1960), p. 27.

the United States are often in conflict. One of the resources which can be drawn upon in such circumstances is public beliefs about who *ought* generally to prevail.

If the effects of the process of development on conceptions of who is important are significant, its effects on partisan motivations are more so. As was suggested earlier in this chapter, the stable attachments of a large proportion of the American electorate to the existing major political parties provide something of a balance wheel to the political system by impeding the rise of new political movements. The stability of voters' party preferences (and the importance of these preferences as a determinant of voting) has the further effect of fostering the long periods in American political history during which one or the other party is generally dominant. Our analysis of the development of partisan motivations helps to provide insight into why generations of voters coming of age in the affluent 1950s and 1960s might be expected faithfully to reproduce voting patterns which have their roots in the experiences of earlier generations with the vicissitudes of the 1930s.

CHAPTER 5

Social Class Differences in Political Learning

There have been countless studies of the connections between social class and *adult* political behavior, and perhaps even more research relating class to *nonpolitical* aspects of child training and development. Thus, although class differences in children's political development have not been studied, a good bit is known about the class setting of American political socialization.

The subdivision of sociology known as social stratification has no shortage of controversies. Scholars disagree about the nature and extent of class differences both in the political behavior of adults and in the training of children. More fundamentally, the importance of class itself as a social phenomenon, its defining characteristics, and the appropriate way to measure it, all have been the subject of extensive debate. Because of this it is easy to forget that there is a good deal of fundamental agreement about social stratification in the United States.

Few would disagree, for example, with Lipset's and Bendix's observations about the universality of class. "In every complex society," they comment,

> there is a division of labor and a hierarchy of prestige. Positions of leadership and social responsibility are usually ranked at the top, and positions requiring long training and superior intelligence are ranked just below. The number of leaders and highly educated individuals constitutes everywhere a small minority. On the other hand, the great majority

is made up of persons in the lower strata who perform manual and routine work of every sort and who command scant
rewards and little prestige.[1]

"Official" rhetoric in the United States does tend to deny the
existence of social classes on this side of the Atlantic, and, in a
sense, the rhetoric is justified: the *term* "class" is not widely used
in popular discourse. Americans seem not to perceive an agreed-
upon set of stratification categories, the way (to take an extreme
example) the members of the Indian caste system perceive a rigid
gradation of merit from Brahmans, through Kshatriyas, Vaisyas,
and Sudras, down to untouchables.

Although most Americans do not perceive their society in a
conscious and explicit class framework, they often use status and
prestige rankings. As we saw in our discussion of popular estimates of the importance of high political leaders (Chapter 3),
there is general consensus on the prestige of occupations. There
seems to be a major division between the social standing of manual (blue-collar) and nonmanual (white-collar) occupations,
roughly the categories we shall be using for analyzing the New
Haven data.[2]

The prestige rankings of occupations are quite highly correlated with other variables which figure in statistical indices of
class level: education; to a somewhat lesser degree, income; possession of the various appurtenances of material prosperity; place

1. Seymour M. Lipset and Reinhard Bendix, *Social Mobility in Industrial
Society* (Berkeley, University of California Press, 1962), p. 1.
2. The following are basic texts and collections of source materials on
social stratification: Joseph A. Kahl, *The American Class Structure* (New York,
Rinehart, 1953); Bernard Barber, *Social Stratification* (New York, Harcourt,
Brace and World, 1957); Leonard Reissman, *Class in American Society* (New
York, The Free Press of Glencoe, 1959); Reinhard Bendix and Seymour Martin
Lipset, *Class, Status, and Power* (Glencoe, The Free Press, 1953). On awareness
of social class see, for example, Richard Centers, *The Psychology of Social
Classes* (Princeton, Princeton University Press, 1949) and Gerhard Lenski,
"American Social Classes: Statistical Strata or Social Groups?" *American
Journal of Sociology, 58* (1962), 139–44. On occupational prestige, see
Albert J. Riess, Jr. et al., *Occupations and Social Status* (New York, The
Free Press of Glencoe, 1961).

of residence in the community. In addition, "members of different social classes, by virtue of enjoying (or suffering) different conditions of life, come to see the world differently—to develop different conceptions of social reality, different aspirations and hopes and fears, different conceptions of the desirable."[3] Therefore it is possible (with some oversimplification) to think of social classes as subcultures, into which people are born and within which they acquire distinctive sets of values. Since the different social strata vary in the kinds of skills as well as the values they apply to political participation, and since they are differentially affected by public policy, it is scarcely surprising that class has a significant impact on politics.[4]

CLASS DIFFERENCES IN THE POLITICAL BEHAVIOR OF ADULTS

We can conveniently distinguish between class differences in *direction* of political participation and class differences in *degree* of participation and involvement. Differences in direction of participation have received the greatest attention, but differences in degree of participation also are important. And it is the latter which are best illuminated by considering the political differences between upper- and lower-status New Haven children.[5]

Direction of participation

Perhaps the most familiar finding of the voting studies is that upper-status Americans tend to support the Republican party, and lower-status people, the Democratic party. Elsewhere in the world similar relationships hold; manual laboring strata are the core voters of reformist, "left" parties; the higher the social stra-

3. Melvin L. Kohn, "Social Class and Parent-Child Relationships: An Interpretation," *American Journal of Sociology,* 68 (1963), 471.

4. Cf. Bernard Berelson et al., *Voting,* pp. 73–75.

5. In analyzing sex differences (Chapter 6), I also shall concentrate on degree rather than direction of participation.

tum the greater the likelihood of supporting conservative parties.[6]

Social class has a somewhat more complex relationship to attitudes than to party support. Lower-status people tend to be "economic liberals"; that is, they favor social welfare programs, policies promoting income equalization, graduated taxation and so forth. They do *not* support "liberal" legislation bearing on civil liberties (e.g. guarantees of free speech to groups such as atheists and communists) and foreign policy (e.g. increased foreign aid). Lower-status people also tend to display "moral conservatism" and traditionalism—for example, they are more ready than people of higher social status to support punitive criminal legislation, strict child-raising, and automatic deference to authority. As the social ladder is ascended, economic liberalism decreases, and liberalism in the civil liberties, foreign policy, and "moral" areas increases.[7] Class differences in party support and political opinion are important sources of the basic divisions in American politics and therefore have a major effect on the political system.

Degree of participation

Class differences in political preference are not, however, directly converted into election results and policy outcomes. The effect of different social class groups on politics is augmented or diminished, among other ways, by the degree to which the groups are politically active. Research findings on class differences in political activity have been quite uniform: the lower an individual is in status the less likely is he to be active and involved—not

6. Seymour M. Lipset et al., "The Psychology of Voting," in *Handbook of Social Psychology, 2,* 1124–75. Early voting research was so much taken with class as a determinant of voting behavior that there was little attention to the possible variations in class cleavage over time and in differing social settings. More recently, with the accumulation of data, including trend data from a number of national presidential election surveys, it has become clear that at least in the United States the relationship between class and voting is quite variable. See Campbell, *The American Voter,* pp. 333–80.

7. See, for example, Key, *Public Opinion and American Democracy,* pp. 121–81.

only in politics, but also in other aspects of community life. Exceptions are rare and occur mainly where the working classes are highly organized (for example, in some European communities), or with respect to specialized activities such as precinct work for urban party organizations. In the contemporary United States, class differences in participation enable the Republican party to compete effectively in national elections even though it commands the allegiance of only about two fifths of the electorate; thus, these differences serve to reduce the impact of the lower strata on public policy.[8]

The lower political participation of the blue-collar strata is a result of numerous situational and psychological determinants. Lane, in a useful summary discussion, deals with factors such as class differences in available leisure and financial resources, in ability to perceive the personal stakes in public policy, in the tendency to belong to organized groups and to have social contacts, and in possession of the sorts of verbal skills which facilitate political participation. Lane also suggests that *"child-rearing practices in the lower-status groups tend to provide a less adequate personality basis for appropriately self-assertive social participation."*[9]

CLASS DIFFERENCES IN CHILD TRAINING AND DEVELOPMENT

Lane summarizes his brief examination of the political significance of class differences in socialization by commenting that, "in general, the middle-class child seems to receive, at the same time, greater encouragement to explore and be ambitious and greater capacity for internal regulation and purposive action."[10] As he points out, much of the literature comparing social classes in their

8. On class differences in participation see Robert E. Lane, *Political Life* (Glencoe, The Free Press, 1959), pp. 45–96 and 220–34 and the sources there cited.

9. Ibid., p. 234. My italics.

10. Ibid., p. 228.

child-training practices is of questionable political relevance. Research has concentrated on a limited range of early socialization practices—on, in Sewell's words, "such aspects of infant discipline as manner of nursing, weaning, scheduling, bowel and bladder training."[11] Later research has failed to demonstrate that differences in these practices are unambiguously related to personality formation.[12]

In spite of the preoccupation with "infant discipline," there gradually has emerged a broader configuration of findings on class differences in socialization—findings which enable us to characterize the nature and consequences of childhood experiences in different socioeconomic settings in the United States. These support and amplify Lane's conclusions.

Two somewhat related clusters of observations in the child development literature help us to understand class differences in the political involvement of New Haven children. These relate to (1) the superior verbal and scholastic capacity of higher-status children, and (2) their markedly greater intellectual and psychic autonomy—their willingness and ability to express feelings and ideas.

1. The higher his social status the more likely a child is to receive superior school grades, to show satisfactory adjustment to the classroom, and to score high on the various tests designed to

11. William H. Sewell, "Social Class and Childhood Personality," *Sociometry, 24* (1961), 350; also see the bibliographical references in this article, p. 340 n. and pp. 354–56.

12. See Sewell, ibid., for a valuable history of research on class and socialization. Much of the early literature was at pains to suggest that the more relaxed weaning-cleaning practices of lower-class families contributed to sounder psychological development than the rigidity of middle-class child-rearing practice. However, the effect of such practices on later development was never established. Later research indicated that lower-class child-training practices were not more easygoing. For an ingenious trend analysis of the child-training studies, suggesting that the seeming contradictions between the earlier and later studies are in fact indications of changing infant care practices but that class differences in the overall climate of child-rearing have remained consistent, see Urie Bronfenbrenner, "Socialization and Social Class Through Time and Space," in *Readings in Social Psychology,* ed. Eleanor E. Maccoby et al. (3d ed. New York, Holt, 1958), pp. 400–25.

measure intelligence. In New Haven, for example, 73 per cent of the upper socioeconomic status children in the present sample, and only 41 per cent of the lower socioeconomic status children, received school grades in the A–B range during the 1956–57 school year. Eighty-seven per cent of the upper-status children and only 59 per cent of the lower-status children received A or B grades for what once was called "deportment." The educational psychology literature amply demonstrates that these are typical findings. And, in spite of heroic efforts to develop intelligence tests which are free of class bias, measures of basic ability also consistently differentiate between socioeconomic groups.[13]

2. If lower-status children are equipped with fewer intellectual skills, they also are equipped with a weaker desire to use such skills. This seems in part to be a function of the general tone of parent–child relationships as they vary by class. There is some evidence that lower-class children enjoy more physical freedom than upper-class children. The former tend to stay up later at night, to be freer in their physical movements in the community, to be less controlled in their peer group activities.[14] But they are granted substantially less "psychological freedom." Upper-status parents take the child's opinions seriously, explain the reasons for parental requirements, and discuss family problems with the child.[15] In general, parent–child relationships are more open, less

13. Useful summary discussions of this literature are: Harold Jones, "The Environment and Mental Development," in *Manual of Child Psychology*, ed. Leonard Carmichael (New York, Wiley, 1954), pp. 631–96; W. B. Brookover and David Gottlieb, "Social Class and Education," in *Readings in the Social Psychology of Education*, ed. W. W. Charters, Jr. and N. L. Gage (Boston, Allyn and Bacon, 1963), pp. 3–11; W. W. Charters, Jr., "Social Class and Intelligence Tests," ibid., pp. 12–21.

14. George Psathas, "Ethnicity, Social Class, and Adolescent Independence from Parental Control," *American Sociological Review, 22* (1957), 415–23. Cf. Robert J. Havighurst and Allison Davis, "A Comparison of the Chicago and Harvard Studies of Social Class Differences in Child Rearing," *American Sociological Review, 20* (1955), 438–42, for instances in which lower-status children seem to enjoy less physical freedom than upper-status children.

15. Psathas, "Ethnicity, Social Class"; Margherita MacDonald et al., "Leisure Activities and the Socio-Economic Status of Children," *American Journal of Sociology, 54* (1949), 505–19.

punitive, and more accommodating to the child's individuality. Maas comments that:

> Lower-class parents are . . . closed or inaccessible to the child's communications, especially of the milder types of disapproval or refusal of parental expectation or demand. Relationships between the parents being hierarchical . . . the child is once removed . . . from direct communication with one parent or the other. Fear of parental authority and its explosive anger mutes the child, until he explodes in a similar manner or redirects his hostile aggressions, as well as his tender feelings, toward siblings or other contemporaries. With them, he may become either a prototype of the bully—status and power seeking—or an ever-submissive follower.

Upper-status parents are more receptive to their children's desires,

> or so the children *feel.* Father and mother, being relatively equal powers in the child's eyes, are equally accessible to him. Socially, they invite him to share their activities . . . Psychologically he seems free to express both positive and negative feelings toward his . . . parents; they . . . modify decisions when the children . . . [seek] extensions of parental limitation.[16]

Kohn, in a recent summary of his own research and earlier studies, observes that

> working-class parents value obedience, neatness, and cleanliness more highly than do middle-class parents, and that middle-class parents in turn value curiosity, happiness, consideration, and—most importantly—self-control more highly than do working-class parents . . . there are characteristic clusters of value choice in the two social classes: working-class parental values center on conformity to external pro-

16. Henry S. Maas, "Some Social Class Differences in the Family Systems and Group Relations of Pre- and Early Adolescents," *Child Development, 22* (1951), 146–52.

scriptions, middle-class parental values on *self*-direction. To working-class parents, it is the overt act that matters: the child should not transgress externally imposed rules; to middle-class parents, it is the child's motives and feelings that matter: the child should govern himself.[17]

Related to the tendency of higher-status parents to encourage an internalized sense of responsibility in their children is the finding in a number of studies that upper-status children are more likely than lower-status children to think and plan in terms of the future; to be able to defer immediate gratifications in order to obtain long-range goals. The differences in "future orientation" extend even to such seemingly trivial realms as whether the child is given music lessons.[18]

Class differences in child training, as Kohn suggests, are understandable in terms of the differences in life styles and requirements of blue- and white-collar existence. Although

there is substantial truth in the characterization of the middle-class way of life as one of great conformity . . . *relative to* the working class, middle-class conditions of life require a more substantial degree of independence of action. Furthermore, the higher levels of education enjoyed by the middle class make possible a degree of internal scrutiny difficult to achieve without the skills in dealing with the abstract that college training sometimes provides. Finally, the economic security of most middle-class occupations, the level of income they provide, the status they confer, allow one to focus his attention on the subjective and the ideational. Middle-class conditions of life both allow and demand a greater degree of self-direction than do those of the working class.[19]

17. "Social Class," p. 475.
18. MacDonald, "Leisure Activities." In the New Haven sample, 54 per cent of the upper-status children and only 21 per cent of the lower-status children reported that they received some sort of lessons (music, dancing, Sunday school, etc.) in addition to their normal school work.
19. Kohn, p. 477.

All of this is certainly relevant to the capacity and desire to raise children who are able to perform the rather intricate manipulations of symbols involved in effective political participation.

CLASS DIFFERENCES IN CHILDREN'S POLITICAL ORIENTATIONS

Some of the items in the New Haven questionnaire did not elicit different responses from children of upper- and lower-status backgrounds. But wherever consistent class differences appeared they showed that upper-status children exceed lower-status children in capacity and motivation for political participation. More important than the mere fact of class differences in political involvement was the *pattern* of these differences. This pattern, as we shall see, is quite consistent with findings in the general literature on class differences in socialization. Considered together, the general socialization literature and the New Haven political socialization findings provide us with some rather precise indications of the ways in which being socialized within a socioeconomic status group affects the individual's later political behavior.

We may note in passing that clear-cut class differences emerged in the New Haven findings even though two aspects of the analytic procedure tend to depress the association between class and political involvement. First, the technique of analyzing findings by school year rather than by chronological age sets up comparisons between groups of slightly unequal ages, since lower-status children are somewhat older (by three to six months) than upper-status children at the same school year level. Analysis by age would presumably have further sharpened the findings pointing to lack of political involvement among lower-status children. Secondly, a necessarily crude technique for measuring class was used: because school records and children's reports proved to be unreliable indicators of parental occupation, social status was measured by drawing upon a block-by-block evaluation of the social level of New Haven neighborhoods based on a then seven-year-old sample of New Haven families. The findings are presented in terms of a rough division between children of blue- and white-collar occupational backgrounds.[20] Neighborhood is not a perfect indicator of class and undoubtedly there had been some changes in the interim between the neighborhood evaluation and the present study. As a consequence, some children probably were in the wrong status group, thus further diminishing the clarity of class differences in the findings.[21] The persistence of these differences in spite of the foregoing analytic deficiencies is evidence of the importance of class as a determinant of political socialization.

Class and orientation toward issue and party

A good bit of the pattern of class differences in children's political orientations becomes evident when we return to the findings reported in Chapter 4 on the development of partisan motivations. Table 4.2 of that chapter, dealing with the development of issue orientation, provides a useful starting point. As we saw, grade school children are not conspicuously issue oriented. Nevertheless, by seventh grade, 32 per cent of the upper-SES children referred at least vaguely to issues in their attempts to distinguish between the parties; by eighth grade, 42 per cent did. Only five per cent of the lower-status seventh graders and 20 per cent of the eighth graders referred to issues.[22] In addition, at

20. For further discussion of the index of social class used here and the class characteristics of the sample see Appendix B.

21. Dichotomizing the class groups also reduces the impression of differences by concealing the responses of children at the very lowest and highest status levels.

22. Significance levels are indicated in footnotes to the appropriate tables in Chapter 4. As indicated in note 2, Chapter 4 and in Appendix B, the data do not meet the requirements of statistical inference and tests have been performed simply to sort out findings for discussion. For the test procedure see the note to Table 4.1. In this and the following chapter, differences are computed by combining chi square values for each age level and computing an overall probability; this makes it possible to avoid discussing occasional inconsistent differences which emerge in specific school-year groups, but which do not appear elsewhere in the data. I have *not* avoided discussing consistent trends in the data (e.g. differences at the .10 level) which do not reach statistical significance.

every age level, the upper-SES children more frequently respond in political terms when asked how they would "change the world." Such responses, as we noted, increase rather sharply between fourth and fifth grade for upper-status children; there is a similar increase among lower-SES children, but it does not appear until a year later.

Children of upper- and lower-status backgrounds also differ in their developing orientations to political parties, as can be seen from one further finding in Table 4.2 and from several observations in Table 4.3 (p. 73). There are no significant differences between the status groups in the mere tendency to possess a party identification[23] (Table 4.3), but the party preferences of upper-status children are better grounded in information. They are more likely to be able to respond to the question asking how the parties differ (Table 4.2) and they are better able to name leaders of the parties (Table 4.3).

One would expect the greater partisan information of upper-status children to augment their capacity to *use* party as an effective tool for making political discriminations and choices. And this seems to be the case. We noted in Chapter 4 that Democratic children tended to evaluate Democratic politicians more favorably than did Republican children and vice versa. This association between party preference and assessment of public officials is stronger for upper- than for lower-status children. In the upper-status subsample, 80 per cent of the children who identified themselves as Republicans rated Eisenhower in the highest category ("very good") and only 37 per cent of the Democrats did so. In the lower-status group, 82 per cent of the Republicans stated that Eisenhower had been doing a "very good job," but so did 68 per cent of the Democrats. Eighty-two per cent of the upper-status Democrats and 42 per cent of the Republicans in this group gave "very good" ratings to New Haven's Democratic mayor; 75 per cent

23. Nor do adults differ in this characteristic. An analysis of the frequency of party identification by various demographic characteristics is presented in Alfred DeGrazia, *The American Way of Government* (New York, Wiley, 1957), pp. 208–09.

of the lower-status Democrats, but also 60 per cent of the lower-status Republicans rated Mayor Lee "very good." This squares with findings on the capacity of adults of different status levels to use their party preferences as a basis for political choice; upper-status adults are more consistently Republican in their voting than are lower-status adults Democratic.

There is a further interesting finding in Table 4.3. At the seventh and eighth grade levels we begin to find upper-status children volunteering the self-designation of "independent" when asked about their party preference. This at first seems paradoxical in view of the keener partisanship of upper-status children. However, the use of the language of nonpartisanship probably does *not* constitute withdrawal from politics by children in this social group. Rather, it fits a pattern which we shall return to later in the present chapter—the tendency for older upper-status children to begin to conceive of politics as a sphere in which it is legitimate and possible to exercise autonomous choice.

Class and information about formal governmental institutions

Another set of responses discussed in Chapter 4—information about formal governmental institutions, as reported in Table 4.1 —fails to vary by socioeconomic status. A total of 75 class comparisons can be made in Table 4.1: we can compare the status groups at each of the five school-year levels in awareness of the names of three executives (the incumbent mayor, governor, and president) and in two levels of familiarity ("reasonably accurate," "aware") with the duties of both the executives and the legislatures. When this is done, no consistent differences emerge; the few statistically significant differences do not regularly favor one group or the other.[24]

24. The absence of class differences in formal political information also is indicated when data from Table 4.1 are combined with a nine-point index of political information (based on "reasonably accurate" descriptions of the six institutions and awareness of the names of the three executives). We shall see in Chapter 6 that this index does differentiate between boys and girls.

Since, as we have seen, there *are* substantial differences in
information about a key *informal* aspect of politics—political
parties—the possibility arises that classroom instruction may have
something to do with equalizing the awareness of formal governmental information. Lessons about "How a Bill Becomes a Law,"
or "What the Mayor Does," are accepted parts of the grade school
curriculum; discussions of partisan politics are less likely to be.
Some aspects of partisanship, for example, the nature of differences between the parties, are probably considered too controversial and "subjective" to be dealt with in the classroom.[25] Therefore, if this information is not learned in the home and neighborhood, it probably is not learned at all early in childhood.

A comparison of political information scores by the various
classrooms from which members of the sample were drawn generally supports the thesis that classroom teaching tends to equal-
ize the information about formal aspects of government among
upper- and lower-status children. For, although government information did not vary by SES, there *were* variations between
classrooms which were generally consistent with impressions
gained from my classroom discussions with children and their
teachers after administering the questionnaire and with reports
of school supervisors as to the teacher's assiduity in teaching current events and social studies.[26]

25. As I have noted, civic instruction is not mandatory before eighth grade
in Connecticut and in New Haven is first suggested as a *possible* topic in the
sixth grade. Teachers vary in their attention to this subject matter. Even discussion of partisanship is not totally absent from the classroom, as we see from
Judith's description of a mock presidential campaign (pp. 19–20). It may be
that partisan information is not presented didactically and therefore that less
of it is remembered.

26. Several items about media information and attention were included in
the study and these, under more satisfactory testing conditions, would probably
have differentiated between upper- and lower-status children. Media items of
the sort used in New Haven, mainly questions about which recent news events
children found interesting, pleasing, and displeasing, are markedly influenced
by temporal events—by the previous day's or week's news. Shortly before
questionnaires were administered in one of the four schools from which
respondents were drawn, a school which is heavily lower class, the United
States succeeded in launching its first successful space satellite. A large pro-

Further class differences in political learning

Table 5.1 reports several additional comparisons between the socioeconomic groups. The first two rows deal with items on children's exemplars: questions about what "famous person you want, or do not want, to be like." This is a portion of the data which we shall analyze further in Chapter 7. Both questions evoke a startling number of references to the heroes of popular culture—actors, actresses, singers, etc. They also bring forth references to public figures past and present, ranging from the incumbent president to the occupants of the gallery of American patriotic heroes and heroines. Upper-status children are more likely to select such public figures as their exemplars. Except in the fourth grade subsample, the class differences are even more clear-cut in the choice of public figures as *negative* exemplars—"people you don't want to be like."

It is interesting to note that the socioeconomic groups do not differ in the two remaining observations in Table 5.1, which involve explicit statements about personal willingness to participate in politics and the "importance" of politics. Both groups are quite likely to say that they will vote when they are of age (almost no children deny that they will vote; the remaining responses are largely "don't know's") and to say that elections are important. These (or their adult equivalents) are items which we expect will vary by socioeconomic status in the general population.[27] Thus,

portion of the children referred to this event, demonstrating that aspects of politics (in this case international politics) can occasionally arouse great enthusiasm among children, but also invalidating socioeconomic status comparisons in the media items. (We shall see in Chapter 6 that the media items do differentiate between the sexes.) Class differences in attention to the political content of the media probably would have appeared if the questionnaires had been administered simultaneously to the entire sample, and at a time when the headlines were not filled with events of such overwhelming interest to *all* children.

27. Gerhard H. Saenger, "Social Status and Political Behavior," in Bendix and Lipset, *Class, Status and Power*, p. 349.

TABLE 5.1. SES Differences and Similarities in Political Response by School Year[a]

	School Year				
	4	5	6	7	8
Names someone from public life as "famous person you want to be like"	Upper SES				
	39%	22%	29%	13%	22%
	Lower SES				
	16	21	16	6	12
Names someone from public life as "famous person you *don't* want to be like"	Upper SES				
	18	32	35	36	32
	Lower SES				
	10	8	15	13	22
Will vote when 21	Upper SES				
	76	82	70	87	86
	Lower SES				
	77	76	79	85	84
Believes "elections are important"	Upper SES				
	63	79	71	69	84
	Lower SES				
	76	66	68	66	75
Total cases	Upper SES				
	49	56	46	38	37
	Lower SES				
	62	62	69	97	143

a. SES differences in choice of a public figure as someone "you *don't* want to be like" are significant (p>.01 <.05). Differences in positive reference to public figures approach significance (p>.05 <.10). On the procedure used for significance testing, see Table 4.1 (p. 58) and Appendix B.

although we have evidence in the New Haven data of the class differences in political involvement and awareness present in the adult population, *the explicit rationalizations which go with low political involvement do not seem to be present by eighth grade.*

So far, we have seen a number of responses which are more often made by upper- than by lower-status children. Tables 5.2

and 5.3 report responses which are more common in the *lower*-status subsample, but which nevertheless reinforce our impression that lower-status children are less politicized than upper-status children.

Table 5.2 compares the status groups in their evaluations of the president, governor, and mayor at the five school-year levels. In 13 of the 15 evaluations (all but the seventh and eighth grade evaluation of the Mayor), lower-status children are more likely to say that the executive has been doing a "very good" job, the highest of the evaluative categories. In Table 5.3, the evaluations by the two oldest age groups of a pair of competing politicians—

TABLE 5.2. Class Differences in Evaluations of Political Leaders by School Year: Leader Rated "Very Good"[a]

			School Year		
	4	5	6	7	8
President			Upper SES		
	79%	68%	54%	51%	53%
			Lower SES		
	82	80	75	77	68
Governor			Upper SES		
	31	37	33	11	36
			Lower SES		
	56	46	40	47	44
Mayor			Upper SES		
	53	59	51	58	64
			Lower SES		
	77	75	66	56	61
Total cases[b]			Upper SES		
	48–49	53–56	44–45	37–38	36
			Lower SES		
	61–62	61	68–69	93–97	139–43

a. SES differences in "very good" evaluations of the governor and president are significant at the .01 level. Differences in "very good" evaluation of the mayor approach significance (p<.10 >.05).

b. Total cases vary due to invalid responses.

Eisenhower and Stevenson—are presented. Lower-status children show a generally more favorable disposition toward *both* men; they are more likely to evaluate both men favorably and less likely to make polar ("very good" or "bad") distinctions between them. These findings are reminiscent of two observations we have already discussed—the reluctance of lower-status children to name politicians as negative exemplars, and the low correlation of their party preferences with their evaluations of leaders.

TABLE 5.3. Class Differences in Comparisons of Eisenhower and Stevenson: Seventh and Eighth Grade Subsample[a]

	Upper SES	Lower SES
Both men rated "high" ("very good" and/or "good")	25%	36%
Both rated "very good"	5	12
Polar: One "very good," one "bad"	10	7
Both rated the same	13	20
No answer	19	27
Total cases[b]	75	243

a. SES differences are not significant when tested by the techniques used here of testing each category of response, combining chi square values (corrected for continuity) for each school year group (in this case, seventh and eighth grades).

b. Percentages in the various categories are neither exhaustive nor mutually exclusive and therefore do not add up to 100 per cent.

In Chapters 3 and 4, I argued that idealization of leaders is an "immature" pattern of political response. Here we see (and the Chicago data also reveal class differences in idealization)[28] that the lower-SES child is in effect more deferential toward leaders than the higher-status child, another indication of less fully developed capacities for political participation.

28. Judith V. Torney, "The Child's Idealization of Authority" (unpublished M.A. thesis, University of Chicago Library, 1962). Mrs. Torney argues the interesting thesis that lower-class children, in their idealization of remote authority figures, are responding in a compensatory fashion to threatening experiences with family authority. Also see note 33, Chapter 3.

Before I attempt to recapitulate and interpret these observations about class differences in political learning, let us consider one further set of findings. The New Haven children were asked

> If you could vote, who would be best to ask for voting
> advice? (*Check one*)
> A friend your own age ....
> Brother or sister ....
> Father ....
> Mother ....
> Teacher ....
> Someone else ....
> (*Write in whether this person is
> a neighbor, relative, or what.*)

Table 5.4 compares the status groups on three categories of response to this item. As might be expected, the bulk of the references were to parents. (Many children did not distinguish between their parents, in spite of instructions to do so.) References to parents diminish with age and two classes of response become more common. The older upper-status children begin to volunteer the statement, which is in no way suggested in the questionnaire, that they would make their *own* choices. Lower-status children, however, virtually never make this statement; instead they refer to the school teacher.

The teacher is probably the one emissary of middle-class subculture with whom many lower-status children are acquainted. One suspects that, since by sixth, seventh, and eighth grades children are well aware of status differences,[29] the lower-class child

29. On awareness of social class by children see Bernice L. Neugarten, "Social Class and Friendship among School Children," *American Journal of Sociology*, 51 (1946), 305–13; Frank J. Estvan, "The Relationship of Social Status, Intelligence and Sex of Ten and Twelve Year-Old Children to an Awareness of Poverty," *Genetic Psychology Monographs*, 46 (1952), 3–60; Benjamin Pope, "Socio-Economic Contrasts in Children's Peer Culture Prestige Values," *Genetic Psychology Monographs*, 48 (1953), 157–220; Hans Schneckenburger, "Das sociale Verständnis des Arbeiterkindes," *Zeitschrift für Pädagogische Psychologie*, 34 (1933), 274–85.

TABLE 5.4. Children's Preferred Sources of Voting Advice by School Year
and Socioeconomic Status[a]

	School Year				
	4	*5*	*6*	*7*	*8*
One or both parents			Upper SES		
	86%	88%	70%	76%	57%
			Lower SES		
	81	74	71	70	63
"Would decide myself"			Upper SES		
(written in)	2	4	11	10	11
			Lower SES		
	0	0	1	3	2
Ask teacher			Upper SES		
	4	2	0	0	11
			Lower SES		
	8	8	16	14	15
Total cases			Upper SES		
	49	56	46	38	37
			Lower SES		
	62	62	69	97	143

a. SES differences in choice of teacher are significant ($p > .01 < .05$). Differences in "decide myself" approach significance ($p < .10 > .05$).

has begun to develop a sense of his own (and his parents') inadequacy in coping with the abstract, the verbal, and the remote—including the symbols of the world of politics. References to the teacher as a preferred source of advice may be the first harbinger of later attitudes which explicitly deny the desirability, appropriateness, and effectiveness of personal political participation.

CAUSES AND CONSEQUENCES OF CLASS DIFFERENCES IN POLITICAL DEVELOPMENT

In general the New Haven findings mesh convincingly with the existing literatures dealing with class differences in adult political participation and children's socialization, providing us with something of a bridge between the two bodies of research.

We find that there are clearly evident pre-adult precursors to the class differences in the political behavior of adults. Lower and upper socioeconomic status children differ in the same ways as do their elders on a good number of the indicators of political awareness and involvement used in New Haven—this in spite of the crudeness of the procedure used for comparing the status groups.

Explanations of the lower political participation of lower-status people vary in the degree to which they emphasize *situational* restraints operating in the individual's adult environment, or *psychological* restraints which he, in effect, brings with him to his adult setting. A situational explanation of lower-class political apathy is suggested by Hyman and Sheatsley. They refer to "families who are weighed down by a pressing burden of personal problems. . . . women who wear themselves out daily with the care of large families in substandard living quarters . . . abject poverty, crushing illness."[30] If the main factors are situational, the solution, as Hyman and Sheatsley point out, is change in the adult's environment: "Sometimes the task is only to free people from their pressing concern with personal problems so that they may have occasional opportunities to look out to broader horizons."[31] But when we find that differences in political involvement already are present in the grade school years, it becomes clear that nonsituational factors—predispositions acquired before the age of formal entrance into citizenship—also are relevant.

Explanations of class differences in participation also may vary in the *depth* of the psychological factors which are said to affect participation. Emphasis may be placed on "surface" factors, of a sort which could be (relatively) easily remedied by increasing an

30. Herbert H. Hyman and Paul B. Sheatsley, "The Current Status of American Public Opinion," *National Council for Social Studies Yearbook, 21* (1950), 11–34, reprinted in *Public Opinion and Propaganda,* ed. Daniel Katz et al., reference at p. 48.

31. Ibid.

individual's education (educational levels *are* rising quite rapidly in the United States), or encouraging him to change consciously held attitudes—such as "voting is a waste of time," or "votes don't really have much of an effect on what politicians do." On the other hand, one may suspect that more fundamental, less readily changed psychological processes are at work—for example, strongly felt beliefs in one's personal inadequacy, deferential tendencies, constricted imagination.

The New Haven data certainly indicate that differences in educational accomplishment and the related differences in intellectual skill make up part of the childhood heritage of the different classes and in this way contribute to political participation differences. But taken with the broader literature on social class and socialization, the New Haven findings also suggest that there are even more deeply imbedded psychological impediments to the participation in politics of lower-status groups. These barriers to participation seem to result from lack of self-direction and self-confidence and from inability and unwillingness to express personal feelings and ideas. It is especially notable that lower socioeconomic status children do not share the explicit unwillingness to participate in politics found among adults of the same background. But they *do* show a greater deference toward political leadership; unlike upper-status children they do not begin to display in sixth, seventh, and eighth grades a sense that political choices are theirs to make—that *their* judgments are worth acting upon. And this seems part of a much larger pattern in the socialization practices of American status groups.

Again we have found that socialization helps to explain the persistence of existing political practices. The findings suggest that participation patterns are rooted in complex social and psychological aspects of the subcultures of the classes. These differences are not likely to yield to simple, straightforward programs of education and reform; instead, fundamental and inevitably slow changes of life styles and values will probably be necessary if differential participation is to disappear.

CHAPTER 6

Sex Differences in Political Learning

Although more than four decades have passed since the Nineteenth Amendment made the political status of women legally identical to that of men, differences persist in the political behavior of the sexes.[1] Sex differences, like class differences, are present in both degree and direction of political behavior. Before looking at the political differences between boys and girls we may briefly consider the nature of adult political sex differences.

DIFFERENCES IN THE POLITICAL BEHAVIOR OF MEN AND WOMEN

The most conspicuous differences between men and women in the direction of their political involvement are in issue positions and candidate choices. Women are less willing to support policies they perceive as warlike or "aggressive"—policies ranging from universal military training to capital punishment. Women have been shown to have greater "moralistic orientation" than men; they are more likely to support sumptuary legislation—for example, restrictions on alcohol consumption and gambling.[2]

---

1. For general discussion of female voting and of political differences, see Harold F. Gosnell, *Democracy: The Threshold of Freedom* (New York, Ronald Press, 1948), Chapter 4; Maurice Duverger, *The Political Role of Women* (Paris, UNESCO, 1955); Robert E. Lane, *Political Life* (Glencoe, The Free Press, 1959), pp. 209–16; Louis Harris, *Is There a Republican Majority?* (New York, Harper, 1954), pp. 104–17.

2. A typical finding is reported in the April 26, 1964, American Institute of Public Opinion release. When asked if they favored state lotteries to raise

Women also seem to be less tolerant of political and religious nonconformity.[3] Discrepancies between the attitudes of men and women may in part account for the recurrent sample survey findings of sex differences in candidate preference. The American Institute of Public Opinion found that women were more favorable to Eisenhower than to Stevenson in 1952 and 1956 and slightly more favorable to Nixon than to Kennedy in 1960. After Kennedy's election, however, he received more female than male support against various hypothetical Republican opponents in the AIPO's "trial heat" polls.[4] Sex differences in candidate choice are of particular interest in view of the Survey Research Center finding that in 1952 more women than men were candidate (rather than party or issue) oriented in making their voting decisions.[5]

Sex differences in degree of political participation are perhaps more striking than the disparities in direction of participation. (In this chapter, as in the previous chapter's discussion of social class, it is differences in degree of involvement which are most illuminated by the New Haven findings.) Women are substantially less likely than men to engage in the whole range of activities available to the politically interested citizen. This includes

revenue for state governments, 56 per cent of the men and only 40 per cent of the women in a national sample responded favorably. For representative instances of sex differences in attitude (in a number of nations) see the various entries reported by sex in Cantril and Strunk, *Public Opinion 1935–1946*, e.g. pp. 106, 172, 740, 833, 968, 972, 1052–54.

3. Samuel A. Stouffer, *Communism, Conformity, and Civil Liberties* (New York, Doubleday, 1955), pp. 131–55.

4. See the AIPO summary release of May 1, 1964. Harris, in *Is There a Republican Majority?*, reports Roper findings indicating that the greater female preference for Eisenhower in 1952 converted a slim margin for the General into a landslide victory. Harris also shows substantial sex differences in response to 1952 campaign issues, with much more female concern with the Korean War and allegations of government corruption. For further sources see Fred I. Greenstein, "Sex-Related Political Differences in Childhood," *Journal of Politics, 23* (1961), 354–55 n.

5. Campbell, *The Voter Decides*, p. 155. Cf. Campbell, *The American Voter*, p. 492 n.

the mere act of voting, although the gap in turnout seems to have been declining in recent years, and it also includes more intense forms of mass participation, such as communicating with elected representatives.[6] Consistent with these participation differences, attitude surveys frequently reveal that women inflate the "no opinion" and "no information" response categories.[7] When women do make political evaluations, they show much less sophistication than men, by the yardstick of the Survey Research Center's index of "level of conceptualization."[8] And the gap between the sexes in mass-level participation is, as a glance through the *United States Government Organization Manual* reminds us, multiplied many times over by vast sex differences in the composition of government officialdom.

Sex differences in participation affect political outcomes in at least two ways. Most obviously, they underrepresent any viewpoints and candidate preferences held disproportionately by women. Because of the way they vary by socioeconomic status, sex differences also may have a selective effect on the political success of particular groups. For example, differences in the electoral turnout of men and women in the United States currently are small or nonexistent in the high-education and high-income groups and much larger in the lower groups.[9] In terms of the contemporary relationship of these factors to party preference, a bonus of votes is thereby provided to the Republican party.

In the past, one factor tending to depress female turnout was the consciously held belief of at least some women that "voting is for men."[10] This belief—when applied to the act of voting—is

6. Lane, *Political Life;* Julian L. Woodward and Elmo Roper, "Political Activity of American Citizens," *American Political Science Review,* 40 (1950), 877; Campbell, *The American Voter,* pp. 483–93.

7. Cantril and Strunk, *Public Opinion,* e.g. pp. 37, 131, 197, 368, 740, 1072.

8. Campbell, *The American Voter,* pp. 491–92.

9. Ibid., pp. 485–89; Lane, p. 214.

10. Lane, pp. 210–11; Charles E. Merriam and Harold F. Gosnell, *Non-Voting: Causes and Methods of Control* (Chicago, University of Chicago Press, 1924), pp. 109–16.

doubtless almost completely absent in the population groups where turnout differences have vanished. Angus Campbell and his associates suggest that, as new conceptions of what is appropriate to the female role spread, sex differences in the willingness to vote may disappear in the remaining population groups.[11]

When types of participation other than the act of voting are considered, however, there still seem to be substantial differences in conceptions of the sexes' political roles. For example, in the early 1950s, when James March asked members of an eastern, suburban League of Women Voters organization and their husbands to rank the most and least appropriate policy areas for that group's agenda, he found striking agreement between the spouses that women might discuss "local government" and "education policy" but that they should not discuss "labor policy" and "tax policy."[12] March's finding of political sex specialization is supported by a recent comparative citizenship study. Cross-sections of the populations of five nations were asked how well they felt they understood local political issues and national issues. In each nation both sexes expressed greater local competence, but in every case there also were sex differences indicating a greater tendency for women to feel competent *only* in the local arena. For example, in the United States 68 per cent of the men and 63 per cent of the women were high in the expression of local understanding. Fifty-six per cent of the men, but only 39 per cent of the women, responded similarly about national issues.[13]

A final indication that women still are not viewed as the political equals of men may be seen in responses to the AIPO's recurrent question: "If your party nominated a generally well-qualified person for President and she happened to be a woman, would you vote for her?" As recently as 1963, 55 per cent of a

11. Campbell, *The American Voter,* p. 485.

12. James G. March, "Husband-Wife Interaction over Political Issues," *Public Opinion Quarterly,* 17 (1953–54), 461–70.

13. The other countries included in this study are Great Britain, Germany, Italy, and Mexico. I am indebted to Gabriel A. Almond and Sidney Verba for making these data available to me. For the full report of their study see *The Civic Culture,* especially Chapter 13.

national sample answered "no." Moreover, seven per cent *fewer* women than men were eager to support a female president.[14]

DIFFERENCES IN THE POLITICAL ORIENTATIONS OF BOYS AND GIRLS

In spite of the paucity of political socialization research, a remarkable amount of data relevant to understanding political sex differences in childhood can be found. Sex differences in social development have been studied in luxuriant detail for more than a half century by educators, psychologists, and other students of child development. Many of these studies are conveniently summarized in Hyman's *Political Socialization.*[15]

Hyman, in his discussion of "precursively political" sex differences, draws upon studies both of specifically political sex differences (for example, differences in political information) and sex differences in behavior which is closely relevant to politics (for example, newspaper reading). Research on politically relevant sex differences is also discussed in the authoritative summary of literature on childhood psychological sex differences by Terman and Tyler.[16] After passing in review a number of findings from these studies, we shall turn to the New Haven findings and, thereafter, place both the New Haven and the earlier research on political sex differences in the broader context of the general "nonpolitical" literature on the psychology of the sexes in childhood.

In reviewing studies of political and politically relevant sex differences it is important to note both the date of field work of the various investigations and the ages of children among whom sex differences have been found. The date of field work is relevant because sex roles have so clearly been in transition in the present

14. AIPO release, October 23, 1963. For trend data on attitudes toward women in public life see Cantril and Strunk, pp. 1052–54.

15. Herbert Hyman, *Political Socialization.*

16. Lewis M. Terman and Leona E. Tyler, "Psychological Sex Differences," in Leonard Carmichael, ed., *Manual of Child Psychology* (2d ed. New York, Wiley, 1954), Chapter 17.

century. In view of the often-remarked convergence of adult sex
roles and the increasing tendency for adults to treat young girls
and boys in the same manner, it cannot be assumed that specifically
political and politically relevant sex differences which existed
fifty years ago are still present.[17] Given our discussion in Chapters
3 and 4 of the importance of early learning, it also is interesting
to note the ages of the children studied. When sex differences
emerge early in life it is likely that these differences reflect deep-
seated cultural themes.

Studies of specifically political responses

The several studies dealing with sex differences in specifically
political responses are mainly investigations of adolescents rather
than younger children. Hyman summarizes a pair of surveys conducted in the 1950s, one of American adolescents and the other
of German adolescents and youths.[18] In the German study, but
not in the American study, there was evidence that females express
less interest in politics than do males. Moreover, the German females were more poorly informed about politics than males; in
this respect the German findings resembled a 1942 American poll
which indicated that teen-age girls knew less about politics than
did boys.[19] Another point at which adolescent political sex differences parallel those found among adults is in the tendency to have

17. See, for example, Margaret Mead, *Male and Female* (New York, Men-
tor, 1955), pp. 208–09; Talcott Parsons, "Age and Sex in the Social Structure
of the United States," *American Sociological Review,* 7 (1942), 604–16; Daniel G. Brown, "Sex Role Development in a Changing Culture," *Psychological
Bulletin, 54* (1958), 232–42.

18. Hyman, pp. 34–35. The former consists of findings from the Purdue
Youth Poll of H. H. Remmers, the latter an EMNID Institute for Opinion
Research survey. Both studies were made in the early 1950s.

19. Ibid., pp. 34–35. *Fortune, 26* (November 1942), 84. For the period of
1932–39, boys exceeded girls nationally in the American Government and
Contemporary Affairs Iowa Every Pupil in High School Achievement tests.
J. B. Stroud and E. F. Lindquist, "Sex Differences in Achievement in the
Elementary and Secondary Schools," *Journal of Educational Psychology, 33*
(1942), 656–67.

political opinions. National surveys of high school students conducted by H. H. Remmers in the 1950s consistently indicated more "no opinion" responses among females.[20] Data also exist showing that as early as preadolescence (sixth grade) there are sex differences in the political information of boys and girls, the latter being less well informed.[21] None of the reports on preadolescents, however, is more recent than the 1920s.

Studies of politically relevant responses

Politically relevant information differences have been found somewhat more recently among preadolescents. In a media behavior study conducted in the late 1930s, Meine found that seventh grade (age 12) boys were better informed than girls about the current news. Meine's data suggested generally that the boys were considerably more attuned to politically relevant communications.[22] Ten years earlier, Johnson had found that by the fifth grade boys were more likely than girls to attend to national news.[23] Similarly, a 1936 media study by Brown of children ranging upward from fifth grade showed that more boys than girls reported listening to radio news programs and broadcasts of political speeches.[24]

Politically relevant sex differences also have been found among

20. H. H. Remmers and D. H. Radler, *The American Teen Ager* (Indianapolis, Bobbs Merrill, 1957), pp. 210–21, report responses to 40 items dealing with "The Bill of Rights, Communism, and Fascism." In this national sample of high school students, the "no opinion" category of response varies by sex for 22 of the items (ignoring differences of less than 3 per cent). In each case, the girls are less likely to have opinions.

21. William Burton, *Children's Civic Information* (Los Angeles, University of Southern California Press, 1936).

22. Frederick J. Meine, "Radio and Press among Young People," in Paul F. Lazarsfeld and Frank N. Stanton, eds., *Radio Research 1941* (New York, Duell, Sloan, and Pearce, 1941).

23. Byron L. Johnson, "Children's Reading Interests as Related to Sex and Year in School," *School Review*, 40 (1932), 257–72.

24. Francis J. Brown, *The Sociology of Childhood* (New York, Prentice-Hall, 1939), p. 328.

young children in a class of investigation which was particularly common during the first two decades of this century and which was "rediscovered" by Hyman—studies of children's exemplars, the people with whom they identify. These studies consistently found, for example, that girls were less likely than boys to identify with political leaders of the past and with other historical characters.[25]

The studies of political and politically relevant behavior summarized above suggest that boys exceed girls in both interest in and information about matters relevant to politics. Two unusual studies of children's familiarity with war, conducted during World War II, suggest the sequence in which these differences develop—*differences in interest precede differences in information.* Preston, who studied the war information level of fourth through eighth grade boys and girls, reported higher male scores.[26] Late in the war a pair of investigators reported a similar study of a small sample of considerably younger (first grade) children. Although only twelve boys and nine girls were studied, the findings were strikingly clear-cut. Neither sex dominated in the meager factual awareness of war at this age, but when asked which of a series of pictures they preferred, nine of the boys and *none* of the girls picked war pictures. Eleven of these six-year-old boys and only two of the girls were described by the authors as "enthusiastic or excited" about the war.[27] After considering the New Haven findings, we shall discuss more fully the implications of this sequence in which differences in interest are followed at a later stage by differences in information.

25. Representative studies in this body of literature are Estelle M. Darrah, "A Study of Children's Ideals," *Popular Science Monthly, 53* (1898), 88–98, and David S. Hill, "Personification of Ideals by Urban Children," *Journal of Social Psychology, 1* (1930), 379–92. These studies are discussed in Hyman, pp. 30–31. I return to them in Chapter 7.

26. Ralph C. Preston, *Children's Reactions to a Contemporary War Situation* (New York, Bureau of Publications, Teachers' College, Columbia University, 1942).

27. Leanna Geddie and Gertrude Hildreth, "Children's Ideas about the War," *Journal of Experimental Education, 13* (1944–45), 92–97.

SEX DIFFERENCES IN THE NEW HAVEN DATA

The child development literature, as we have seen, reveals many indications that at least in the past adult sex differences in political behavior had roots in rather early pre-adult differences. But the literature gives no indication of whether this is true of contemporary children, especially the younger age groups.

Table 6.1 compares the sexes in a number of political and politically relevant responses. We see that sex differences in political response, of the same sort which have been reported since the turn of the century, were still present in 1958 in this group of urban, northern children. Wherever the questionnaire responses differentiate between boys and girls, the former are invariably "more political." This is so in the case both of statistically significant sex differences and of nonsignificant differences which exceed two or three per cent. In view of our interest in the age at which differences emerge, Table 6.1 also reports findings for the youngest subgroup of the sample. Similar differences, of roughly the same percentage strength, are present in this subsample of nine-year-olds, although probably because of the much smaller number of cases only one of the fourth grade sex differences is significant.

More specifically, the following observations may be made in connection with Table 6.1.

Specifically political responses

The first entry in Table 6.1 is a political information score consisting of the number of "reasonably accurate" answers to the nine information items asking for the names of the incumbent mayor, governor, and president, descriptions of their duties, and descriptions of the duties of the legislative bodies at each level of government.[28] The fourth grade average score on this index was about three points, two of which in almost every case were

28. To determine the internal consistency of the index, point biserial coefficients of correlation were computed, testing the relationship between cor-

earned by naming the president and New Haven's popular mayor. As we saw in Chapter 4, the amount of political information held by children of this age is infinitesimal. Even so, at the fourth grade level as well as for the total sample, boys were significantly better informed than girls. Further evidence along the same line is provided by the second item in Table 6.1, showing a tendency toward sex differences in ability to name at least one leader of the Republican or Democratic party. An additional "precursive form of politics" which varied by sex was response to the item, "If you could change the world in any way you wanted, what change would you make?" Responses classified as "political" were more frequent among boys. Girls were more likely not to respond at all or to suggest a distinctly nonpolitical change, such as, "Get rid of all the criminals and bad people."

Table 6.1 shows, however, that no sex differences were evoked by the pair of items designed to tap juvenile conceptions of citizen duty and political efficacy: "Will you vote when you are 21?" and "Do you think it makes much difference which side wins an election?" This is not overly surprising. These questions, with their implication of a moral imperative, might if anything have been expected to differentiate between the sexes in the opposite direction, with more favorable replies from girls than from boys.

Politically relevant responses

Distinct, consistently significant differences in media behavior, corroborating findings of the older studies, were found in the New Haven group. Boys were more likely to be able to name a news story in response to an open-ended question which asked the child to describe "a news story which interested you." They also were more likely to answer similar items designed to tap

---

rect responses on each item and the nine-point index composed of these scores. Seven of the items show correlations ranging from .59 to .64, and the remaining two (the president's and mayor's names) were slightly positively correlated (.26 and .22 respectively).

TABLE 6.1. Sex Differences in Political Responses: Fourth Graders and
Total New Haven Sample

Questionnaire items	*Fourth grade subsample*		*Total sample (Grades 4–8)*	
	Boys	*Girls*	*Boys*	*Girls*
SPECIFICALLY POLITICAL RESPONSES:				
Political information score	3.30	2.77**	4.69	4.31*
Can name at least one party leader	41%	33%	56%	48%
Proposes "political" change in the world	13%	5%	41%	34%
Will vote when 21	76%	77%	80%	81%
Believes "elections are important"	69%	72%	72%	73%
POLITICALLY RELEVANT RESPONSES:				
Names interesting news story	65%	47%	73%	60%*
Story named is political	15%	12%	36%	12%*
Names pleasant news story	39%	28%	54%	41%*
Story named is political	9%	2%	26%	17%*
Names unpleasant news story	37%	35%	53%	43%**
Story named is political	18%	9%	33%	20%*
Prefers Washington to New Haven news	52%	35%	38%	26%*
Names someone from public life as "famous person you want to be like"	39%	23%	24%	15%
Names someone from public life as "famous person you *don't* want to be like"	22%	14%	32%	13%*
Total cases	54	57	337	332

*One asterisk indicates that a sex difference is significant at the one per cent level; two asterisks at the five per cent level. The significance of political information score differences was tested with a one-tailed t-test on the basis of a prediction, stemming from the literature summarized in this chapter, that boys would be better informed than girls. All of the percentage differences in the remainder of the table were tested by chi square. For two items summarized in this table the number of cases falls below the number indicated in the total row due to invalid responses. The "Washington news" item is based on 48 boys and 54 girls in the fourth grade subsample and 325 boys and 312 girls in the total sample. The information score for boys in the total sample column is based on 336 instead of 337 cases.

emotional involvement in the news ("Can you think of a news story which made you feel happy? angry?"). In response to these three items, significantly more boys than girls referred to political news.[29] Furthermore, New Haven children resembled Johnson's 1929 sample in the greater male interest in national news.[30]

Nonsignificant sex differences in the same direction were produced by an item resembling the earlier studies of children's identifications ("Name a famous person you want to be like"). This item stimulated nine per cent more boys than girls to refer to figures from "public life," a category including past and present political leaders. The companion item, asking "Name a famous person you *don't* want to be like," produced statistically significant sex differences, with girls about 20 per cent less likely to name a "public life" figure.

In view of the way adult sex differences in electoral participation vary by social status, it might be suspected that the political and politically relevant pre-adult differences reported here are confined to lower socioeconomic status children. This expectation, however, turns out not to be true. When class is controlled, one of the sex differences in Table 6.1 "washes out"; only the lower-SES children vary in the tendency to wish for political changes in the world. But the other eleven differences reported in this table persist.

CAUSES AND CONSEQUENCES OF SEX DIFFERENCES IN CHILDREN'S POLITICAL ORIENTATIONS

The sources of political differences between boys and girls

How can we explain the existence of political sex differences among contemporary grade school children? The discussion of adult sex differences suggests that the first place to look for an explanation is in people's sex role conceptions, their view of the

29. A rather broad class of responses was classified under the heading "political," the most common being references to news stories about satellite competition between the United States and the Soviet Union.

30. See note 23.

TABLE 6.2. Parent Chosen as Preferred Source of Voting Advice, by Sex and School Year*

School year	Boys Father	Boys Mother	Girls Father	Girls Mother	Total cases Boys	Total cases Girls
4	54%	15%	35%	44%	54	57
5	44	10	46	24	61	57
6	53	4	43	22	57	58
7	51	11	31	24	73	72
8	42	11	35	16	92	88
Total	48	10	40	25	337	332

*Based on the check list item reported on p. 103 above. For both boys and girls the percentage differences reported in the total row are statistically significant. The male differences also are significant at each age level, but at the individual age levels only the eighth grade female differences are significant. It should be noted that in spite of the general tendency to recognize the father as the source of voting advice, sex differences exist. Girls choose the mother more often than do boys, and boys exceed girls in references to the father.

kinds of political acts which are appropriately male or female. Perhaps it is common for the young child to acquire the assumption that "politics is the man's business."

Table 6.2 suggests that some sort of awareness of politics as an area of male specialization develops during childhood. This table reports the proportions of children who checked "mother" and "father" in response to the voting advice item. Children of both sexes were more likely to choose the father than the mother as an appropriate source of voting advice.[31] This finding jibes with recurrent reports in the voting literature of male political dominance in the family.[32]

31. It is not likely that these choices simply reflect a greater fondness for the father, since investigations of children's preferences for one or the other parent regularly have found that children say they "like" their mothers more. Terman and Tyler, "Psychological Sex Differences," p. 1101.

32. E.g. Paul F. Lazarsfeld et al., *The People's Choice* (2d ed. New York, Columbia University Press, 1948), pp. 140–45. But Hyman (*Political Socialization,* pp. 83–84) points out the presently inconclusive state of the literature on intrafamily political influence.

The child's awareness of male political specialization is, however, surely not a sole determinant of childhood political sex differences. For this to be the case, we would have to explain the fact that a nine-year-old female is less politically involved than a male of the same age in terms of a conscious deflection of the girl's vision from political events out of the belief that "this is not for girls." Young children are too politically unaware for this to be the case, although, as the interview with Judith suggests, at least tacit notions of this sort seem to develop quite early. (Judith explains why she was for Adlai Stevenson in 1956 by saying, "My father was a Democrat so we stuck with him.")

It is instructive to go beyond children's explicit political perceptions and consider the larger context of experiences and activities which engage the bulk of their attention—their relationships with adults and peers of the immediate environment and their everyday obligations and amusements. In the vast literature on sex differences in childhood "nonpolitics," there are numerous reports of psychological differences, some of which are present almost from the cradle and many of which are stronger than the political differences. For a thorough review of this literature the reader is referred to Terman and Tyler.[33] Here we shall consider three of the bodies of research summarized in their excellent account, looking briefly at studies of "aggressiveness" and "sociability," and considering at greater length an interrelated collection of investigations dealing with childhood sex differences in interests and in spheres of competence.

One psychological dimension along which the sexes vary nonpolitically is in "aggressive and dominant behavior." The far greater prominence of the male in police-blotter and juvenile court statistics is sufficient to remind us that there are great adult and adolescent sex differences in the willingness to express hostility.[34] But it is less well known that differences in aggressiveness emerge almost as soon as children are able to engage in social

33. See note 16.

34. Terman and Tyler, pp. 1085–89. Also John P. Scott, *Aggression* (Chicago, University of Chicago Press, 1958), Chapter 4.

activity. At every age boys are more pugnacious and quarrelsome than girls. Even among the two- to four-and-a-half-year-old nursery-school children studied by Hattwick, boys exceeded girls "in all forms of aggressive behavior with the exception of verbal bossing."[35] This class of sex difference seems to have an obvious bearing on the above-mentioned adult tendencies for women to be more pacifist in their issue positions. In a field as controversial as politics, it also seems possible that differential aggressiveness would affect degree of participation.

Another psychological sex difference which has been observed among children of widely diverging ages confirms the "common belief that one of the characteristically feminine traits is an absorbing interest in persons and personal relations."[36] Terman and Tyler document this assertion with a remarkably disparate set of indices: "sociability ratings" of the kinds of games children prefer, children's references to their worries, and even the content of their dreams.[37] When one reads of this class of childhood sex differences, it is difficult not to be reminded that among adults women are more likely than men to be candidate-oriented.[38]

"Evidence for differences in interests" between boys and girls, Terman and Tyler comment, "is unequivocal. Furthermore, such differences show up with as much clarity in the primary and pre-

35. Terman and Tyler, p. 1086; LaBerta A. Hattwick, "Sex Differences in Behavior of Nursery School Children," *Child Development, 8* (1937), 343–55. Because sex differences in aggressiveness emerge so early there is some tendency to relate them to the manifold physical sex differences which are present from birth, "for almost every physical variable" (e.g. strength, body size, capacity, rate of maturation, and stability of body functions). Terman and Tyler, pp. 1064–67. However, Robert Sears and his associates have shown that the greater aggressiveness of even young boys seems to a considerable extent to be learned. In large part their learning may be through the mechanism of identification with the father. Robert R. Sears, et al., "Effect of Father Separation on Pre-School Children's Doll Play Aggression," *Child Development, 17* (1946), 219–43. Cf. Margaret Mead, *Sex and Temperament in Three Primitive Societies* (New York, Morrow, 1939).

36. Terman and Tyler, p. 1095.

37. Ibid., pp. 1095–96.

38. See note 5.

school groups as in those approaching adulthood."[39] Of the variety they discuss, two types of studies of interest differences, which may at first seem unconnected, are worth juxtaposing: studies of the play and game preferences of preschool children and studies of the reading and school-subject preferences of older children. Together they contribute to an understanding of the developmental processes through which nonpolitical sex differences seem to shape the political.

Children's games are probably much more than indicators of their interests; they also seem to be a part of the process which shapes these interests. It has been argued that through playing the child learns his own identity, since to a notable degree children play at adult roles or idealizations of adult roles.[40] An ingenious procedure to establish the ages at which children's play begins to reflect adult sex roles, making use of a collection of "male" and "female" toys, was devised by Rabban.[41] Sometime between the ages of three and four, Rabban found, children begin concentrating on "sex appropriate" toys as preferred playthings; within a year or two there is almost no deviation from choice by girls of toys symbolic of the home and femininity (e.g. a doll, a bathinette, and a purse) and by boys of toys reflecting male activities out of the home (e.g. soldiers, a steam roller, and a fire engine).

Differences between the sexes in reading interests, Terman and Tyler comment, are

> among the most interesting to be found in any field, because of the clear indication they give of a fundamental difference in masculine and feminine interests. At home, at school, and in the public libraries the books to which children are exposed are largely the same for boys and girls; yet marked

39. Terman and Tyler, p. 1075.

40. Ibid., pp. 1075–78. Cf. George Herbert Mead, *Mind, Self and Society* (Chicago, University of Chicago Press, 1934), pp. 50 ff.

41. Meyer Rabban, "Sex-Role Identification in Young Children in Two Diverse Social Groups," *Genetic Psychology Monograph, 42* (1950), 81–158.

sex differences in reading preferences are evident as early as the primary school grades and persist to the adult years.[42]

Like the toy choices of preschool children, the reading choices of school children vary along the axis of female emphasis on the immediate circle ("milder stories of home and school") and male focus outward into the wider environment ("violent or outdoor adventure, sports, travel, exploration, and war"). Among groups of older school children, the same differences seem to be reflected in the many findings, some of them (as Hyman points out) going back to the late nineteenth century, showing that girls are more likely to read fiction and boys are more likely to read biography and history.[43]

Complementing the sex differences in reading interests, as one might expect, are differences in school-subject preferences. Girls lean toward English and foreign languages; boys prefer the civics–history–social studies complex, as well as science. Moreover, these motivational differences have an interesting effect on the usual relationship between male and female school achievement. It has been uniformly observed that in grade school and high school girls receive higher marks than boys, but in the areas which interest them boys reverse this tendency.[44] The sequence from

42. Terman and Tyler, p. 1078.

43. Ibid., pp. 1078–81; Hyman, pp. 21–33. It should be added that evidence showing female concentration on the immediate environment and male on the wider environment is not confined to studies of children's play and of children's reading. For example, it was regularly reported in the studies of children's identifications discussed above (note 25) that girls were more likely than boys to identify with "acquaintance ideals"—family, neighbors, friends, etc. A number of studies of college students and other groups of older respondents, which show that women are more closely attached to their parents than are men, have been summarized by Mirra Komarovsky. "Functional Analysis of Sex Roles," *American Sociological Review*, 15 (1950), 508–16.

44. For discussion of sex differences and similarities in general intelligence, academic achievement, and academic interests, see Terman and Tyler, pp. 1067–75 and 1081–82. Also Beth L. Wellman, "Sex Differences," in *A Handbook of Child Psychology*, ed. Carl Murchison (2d ed. Worcester, Clark University Press, 1933), Chapter 15. The New Haven findings agree with the general literature on these points: there were no sex differences in general

early sex-based differences in interest to later differences in competence has been best brought out in connection with the field of science. During the early school years there are no differences between boys and girls in aptitudes and abilities related to science. But by the high school level, presumably spurred by the maleness of scientific, engineering, and mechanical pursuits in the United States, differences are so great that the following situation obtains:

> In the Science Talent Search, every year from two to three times as many boys as girls apply, which might lead one to expect that the girls would be more highly selected. Yet, in spite of this fact, the boys have each year obtained higher scores on the test. Differences are unquestionably significant and always in the same direction.[45]

This sequence dovetails closely, of course, with the findings summarized above (p. 114) about how sex differences seem to develop in the politically relevant variable of information about war.

Parallels like these help to explain early sex differences in the political responses of young children, even though politics is a minute part of children's world views. It is only a short step from the variations between the sexes in their interest in social studies and their civics grades to the greater political information of young boys. The step is slightly but not much longer from reading stories about the Wild West, rather than stories about home life, to interest in Washington news rather than New Haven news. Both of these steps seem to be related to the general nonpolitical division of labor between the sexes in American society and to

---

intelligence; girls had significantly higher school grades than boys; boys were significantly more likely to prefer social studies as a school subject than were girls. I have no data on boys' social studies grades. That, in the face of their generally poorer academic performance, boys are better informed politically is, however, especially clear evidence that politics becomes a male specialization at an early age.

45. Terman and Tyler, p. 1072.

the early learning of this division as manifested in the five-year-old boy's insistence on playing with a toy soldier or fire engine, and the girl's selection of a doll.

The political differences between boys and girls do not seem to flow mainly from a rationalistic developmental sequence in which the girl learns "politics is not for girls," hence "I am not interested in politics." Rather there is a much more subtle and complex process in which—through differential opportunities, rewards, and punishments which vary by sex, and by identification with one or the other parent—a sex identity is acquired. Among other things this learning process associates girls with the immediate environment and boys with the wider environment. Political responses, developing as they do relatively late in childhood, fall into the framework of already present nonpolitical orientations.[46]

The effects of childhood sex differences

What do these observations on pre-adult sex differences tell us about the adult phenomenon? The differences in the political behavior of men and women (like the political differences between social classes, which we considered in Chapter 5) have been explained at a number of levels. Some explanations suggest that political sex differences are at least in part based on superficial situational factors which may be easily remedied. The classic nonvoting study of Merriam and Gosnell indicated that the need to stay at home and care for sick members of the family kept a few women from voting.[47] Similarly, the authors of *The American*

46. The belief that politics is not part of the female role may, however, help to reinforce political sex differentiation. This would be especially true later in childhood, as political awareness becomes more fully developed and it becomes possible for the child consciously to accept or reject communications because they are political.

Reinforcement of political sex differences also may be encouraged by the mechanism of identification with figures in the wider environment, combined with the greater availability of male political exemplars for boys than of female political exemplars for girls.

47. *Non-Voting*, pp. 72–77.

Voter, explaining the fact that young women are somewhat more likely to turn out if they have no children, assert: "The presence of young children requiring constant attention serves as a barrier to the voting act."[48] A second level of explanation of political sex differences stresses aspects of the present and past experiences of adults. Gosnell, for example, seems to imply that differences in formal education are the major determinant of political differences.[49] Finally, some explanations dwell on much less malleable psychological causes of political differences, such as the "vestigial" yet "deeply ingrained" sex roles discussed by Campbell and associates,[50] and the female "feeling of dependence on man" described in Duverger's charmingly Gallic remarks.[51] Data based on observations of children do not enable us to come to any final conclusions about the relative weight of explanatory factors at these various levels, but do make it possible for us to reject inadequate theories.

The present data cast particular doubt on theories which suggest that political sex differences will disappear in the near future, on the assumption that such differences derive mainly from the individual's adult experiences. As we have seen, these differences emerge early in life, even in a group of contemporary children, the youngest of whom will not enter the electorate until 1970. Fourth grade political sex differences are patently a consequence neither of situational impediments nor of educational differences, nor, for that matter, of any of the other experiential variables which are held constant by studying the populations of coeducational grade schools. An adequate theory, these data indicate, must

48. Campbell, *The American Voter,* p. 488. This difference could also be explained, however, by other differences between mothers and non-mothers, even within the same educational and socioeconomic stratum.

49. *Democracy: The Threshold of Freedom,* p. 77.

50. Campbell, *The American Voter,* pp. 484–85.

51. Duverger, *The Political Role of Women,* p. 129. "While women have, legally, ceased to be minors," Duverger comments, "they still have the mentality of minors in many fields and, particularly in politics, they usually accept paternalism on the part of men. The man—husband, fiancé, lover, or myth— is the mediator between them and the political world."

account for the psychological underpinnings of political sex differences, understood in terms of sex roles in the society, how they develop, and what maintains them.

Further research is needed to discover just what these underpinnings are. In part they may be curiosity, interest, and other related positive drives, channeled from a tender age in one direction for girls and in another for boys. Politics, although not of deep interest to children of either sex, is more resonant with the "natural" enthusiasms of boys. Other psychological bases also will be found. For example, the need to conform to cultural definitions of masculinity often is bulwarked by powerful feelings. This need is complemented by the severe penalties which departure from the cultural definitions may bring. Women who find it especially threatening not to be "feminine," and who see politics as a male function, will be drawn into the political arena only at the cost of great psychic discomfort.[52]

Many elements in contemporary society counteract the tendency for early learning to perpetuate political sex differences. Women are thrust into the wider environment by their careers, their education, and many other forces, including the proselytizing of political parties. Nevertheless, the aspects of children's political and nonpolitical development described here make it clear that political sex differences, like the class differences discussed in the previous chapter, are unlikely to vanish soon.

52. For evidence that strict adherence to "sex appropriate" roles still carried a strong emotional charge in the 1950s, see the interviews with a pair of Boston area mothers who were rated "high" in "sex role differentiation," reported in Robert R. Sears, et al., *Patterns of Child Rearing* (Evanston, Row, Peterson, 1957), p. 398.

CHAPTER 7

Long-Term Change in Political Learning

We now shift perspective from learning which seems to encourage the persistence of existing patterns of political behavior from generation to generation and consider an instance of long-term, historical *change* in children's learning. So far we have seen that political participation differences between adult men and women and between adults of high and low social status continue to be reflected in the current generation of children, that the older generation's party preferences are passed on to the succeeding generation. Indeed, the socialization process seems to reinforce and strengthen the status quo.

Yet change is ever present in politics. Even as stable a fixture as the American political system itself is constantly being reshaped. The past half century has seen the rise of institutionalized presidential leadership, an apparent increase in the national scope of the party system, and countless other changes. With the accumulation since the 1930s of public opinion poll data, we have begun to acquire firm knowledge of trends in the acquisition of political beliefs among adults. Sometimes adult political learning is glacially slow, sometimes it is rapid, and occasionally slow and rapid patterns alternate. Thus, during the twenty years from 1940 to 1960, the proportion of Americans willing to vote for a "well-qualified" Roman Catholic for president slowly increased by nine per cent (from 62 per cent to 71 per cent); within several months after the election in 1960 of the nation's first Catholic president, the percentage spurted upward by an additional eleven per cent.[1]

1. American Institute of Public Opinion release, September 24, 1961.

Even more dramatic changes presumably take place in less stable political systems. It seems certain, for example, that massive political learning at all age levels and in all segments of the population has occurred in Germany and Japan since World War II.

The discussion in this chapter of long-term changes in learning draws upon a number of forgotten studies of children's attitudes, which enable us to trace a trend line connecting a portion of the New Haven data to findings made as long ago as the turn of the century. The resulting time series makes it possible to document changes over the years in children's orientations; in spite of our emphasis so far on the conservative results of socialization, the content of children's learning does shift with time. Curiously, our findings mainly serve the negative function of casting doubt upon a widely held hypothesis about the ways in which the values learned by children have changed in the present century. The positive significance of the findings we shall be discussing is elusive. Even this elusiveness is of some interest, however, since it suggests certain of the requirements that will have to be met if we are to gather satisfactory trend data on political socialization.

THE DATA ON TRENDS IN CHILDREN'S LEARNING

In the course of analyzing the New Haven data I came upon a number of studies, reported between 1896 and the mid-1940s, of children's exemplars—of their statements about the person "you would most like to resemble." As it turned out, a series of such studies had been reported, largely in education journals, during the decade and a half surrounding the turn of the century; further reports had appeared in the 1920s and in the immediate post-World War II period. In addition, one of the New Haven questionnaire items was quite similar to the items used in the earlier studies.[2]

2. This chapter draws mainly on the studies indicated with asterisks below. Following each in parentheses is the estimated or actual date of field work. In the text these studies are indicated by date of field work rather than date of publication.

*Estelle M. Darrah, "A Study of Children's Ideals," *Popular Science Monthly*,

Thus evidence was available over a fifty-year period of trends in juvenile heroes and hero worship. Several factors made possible the use of data from a period before acceptable standards for survey research had been developed. First, although not based on random sampling, the studies drew on exceedingly large and diversified populations of children. For both ends of the time series, the pre-World War I and the post-1944 periods, several studies were available from widely dispersed geographical areas, and for both of these periods there was enough impressionistic information about respondents' social characteristics to make it clear that the populations studied were broadly heterogeneous. Secondly, raw data were available from five of the studies—two from the early period, one from the 1920s, and two (including the New Haven study) from the later period—making possible

---

53 (May, 1898), 88–98 (Field work 1896); Earl Barnes, "Type Study on Ideals," *Studies in Education*, 2 (1902), 36–42, 78–82, 115–22, 157–62, 198–202, 237–42; *Will G. Chambers, "The Evolution of Ideals," *The Pedagogical Seminary*, 10 (March 1903), 101–43 (Field work c. May 1902); *David S. Hill, "Comparative Study of Children's Ideals," *Pedagogical Seminary*, 18 (June 1911), 219–31 (Field work c. 1910); *David S. Hill, "Personification of Ideals by Urban Children," *Journal of Social Psychology*, 1 (August 1930), 379–93 (Field work c. 1928); *M. Louise Stoughton and Alice M. Ray, "A Study of Children's Heroes and Ideals," *The Journal of Experimental Education*, 15 (December 1946), 156–60 (Field work c. 1944); Robert J. Havighurst et al., "The Development of the Ideal Self in Childhood and Adolescence," *Journal of Educational Research*, 40 (December 1946), 241–57; J. B. Winkler, "Age Trends and Sex Differences in the Wishes, Identifications, Activities, and Fears of Children," *Child Development*, 20 (1949), 191–200; and the New Haven study (Field work January through March, 1958).

Chambers presents a bibliography of a number of additional early studies. Not considered in the present discussion are several early studies of the "ideals" of foreign children, most of which are cited in Chambers' bibliography, and a study of parochial school children by Sister Mary Inez Phelan, *An Empirical Study of the Ideals of Adolescent Boys and Girls* (Washington, Catholic University of America, 1936). A discussion of the findings in several of the early studies with respect to sex differences appears in Hyman, *Political Socialization*, pp. 30–31. These studies first came to my attention through Hyman's references to several of them.

secondary analysis in terms of categories which are more revealing than those used in the original studies. In these five studies complete or nearly complete inventories of all the individuals referred to by the respondents were reported. Therefore reanalysis was possible once the identities of some of the more obscure names (ranging from turn-of-the-century congressmen to silent screen performers) were established and a number of minor estimates made to fill in slight gaps. Finally, the pattern of findings emerging from all the studies was sufficiently clear-cut and internally consistent to eliminate doubts about the representativeness of the data.

Table 7.1 (p. 138) summarizes the findings of the five studies of children's exemplars which were suitable for retabulation. The first four (as well as the other early studies referred to in the text and notes) employed the following item, or some slight variation thereof: "Of all persons whom you have heard, or read about, or seen, whom would you most care to be like or resemble?"[3] The New Haven study used a somewhat different question: "Name a famous person you want to be like."

About one fifth to two fifths of the respondents to the earlier item referred to figures from the immediate environment; the item used in 1958 produced very few such references. Therefore, the latter wording may inflate the proportion of children referring to public figures, although in 1958 failure to respond at all to the item is much more common than in the earlier studies. However, for the analysis which follows, the variation in item and response pattern is not a serious drawback.

3. This is the wording used by Hill, "Personification of Ideals by Urban Children." The item was worded as follows in the other studies: "What person of whom you have heard or read would you most like to be? Why?" (Chambers); "Which person (among those you have seen, or thought of, or heard of, or read about) would you most like to resemble? Why?" (Hill, "Comparative Study of Children's Ideals"); "Of all the persons whom you have known, or heard about, or read about, whom would you most wish to be like? And why do you like this person?" (Stoughton and Ray).

THE LITERATURE ON CHANGE AND CONTINUITY IN AMERICAN VALUES

I have organized the data in Table 7.1 so as to confront an especially pervasive hypothesis, probably best typified in the work of David Riesman, about changes in the values which Americans accept and transmit to their children.

Before analyzing Table 7.1, it will be necessary to examine this hypothesis, and certain evidence which has been advanced in support of it, in some detail. American values, it is claimed, have changed radically since the turn of the century. Americans have come to prize *leisure* over *work, accommodation* to their fellows over individual *achievement;* in general, it is implied that there has been an increasing disposition toward *passivity* rather than *activity.* Riesman's statement of this thesis, which he develops in part by extensive reference to changing socialization practices, is in terms of changes in social structure and "social character"; changes from an "age of production" to an "age of consumption," which he believes has been accompanied by a shift from "inner-" to "other-direction" in the sources of Americans' "modes of conformity."[4] William Whyte's[5] well-publicized comments on "The Declining Protestant Ethic" parallel Riesman's assertions at many points.

The views of Riesman and Whyte are widely accepted. Clyde Kluckhohn reaches similar though not identical conclusions on the basis of a "massive" review of several hundred "empirical and impressionistic writings on American culture and especially

4. David Riesman with Nathan Glazer and Reuel Denney, *The Lonely Crowd: A Study of the Changing American Character* (New Haven, Yale University Press, 1950), hereafter attributed for the sake of brevity to the senior author. A number of commentators on Riesman's work have pointed out that his discussion is less of changing character than of changing values and practices. See, for example, the articles by Sheldon L. Messinger and Burton R. Clark and by Robert Gutman and Dennis Wrong in Seymour M. Lipset and Leo Lowenthal, eds., *Culture and Social Character: The Work of David Riesman* (New York, The Free Press of Glencoe, 1961).

5. *The Organization Man* (New York, Simon and Schuster, 1956).

American values by social scientists and others." Much of the
literature Kluckhohn was able to find had been "produced by
writers . . . who based their reflections on their own experience
rather than upon specifically pointed and systematic research."
Granting that these observations did not meet satisfactory standards of evidence, Kluckhohn nevertheless was impressed by the
amount of broad agreement with Riesman and Whyte, although
he felt it necessary to point to "the possibility that the consonance
derives from *Zeitgeist* or from parrotings—with variations—of
a few popular formulations."[6]

In addition to impressionistic accounts of changing American
values, Kluckhohn was able to draw upon several studies which
presented "hard" data—analyses of various indirect indices of
value change, such as the variations over the years in the content
of the lyrics of popular songs, best selling novels, and religious
literature. The findings of a number of these studies seem to support the assertions of Riesman and Whyte. For example, after
observing differences in the types of individuals who served as
topics of popular magazine biographies between 1901 and 1941,
Leo Lowenthal concluded that contemporary audiences were being
exposed to "idols of consumption" (individuals engaged in con-
sumer service activities, especially entertainers) rather than the
"idols of production" (such as business magnates) of earlier
years.[7] Lowenthal's findings were drawn upon by Riesman to
support the thesis of *The Lonely Crowd*. A more recent example
of the analysis of value changes in cultural products is the study
by deCharms and Moeller of the content over the past century
and a half of grade school textbooks. Noting that "achievement
imagery" in children's readers had declined consistently after the
1880s, deCharms and Moeller concluded that their findings "cor-

6. "Have There Been Discernible Shifts in American Values During the
Past Generation?" in Elting E. Morison, ed., *The American Style* (New York,
Harper and Brothers, 1958), 145–217.

7. Leo Lowenthal, "Biographies in Popular Magazines," in Paul F. Lazarsfeld and Frank N. Stanton, eds., *Radio Research 1942–43* (New York, Duell,
Sloan and Pearce, 1944), 507–48.

respond very well" with those of Riesman and other commentators.[8]

Lately, however, objections have been raised to the argument
that one of the major twentieth-century developments has been
the supplanting of the Protestant Ethic with what Whyte calls
"the Social Ethic." Lipset, for example, after a detailed examination of comments on the United States by nineteenth-century
foreign visitors, asserts that the "traits of the other-directed man
have to a considerable extent always existed in the American
character and that the values of achievement and individualism
persist in American Society."[9] Parsons and White argue that the
American "value-system has . . . remained stable . . ." and that
"a major part of the phenomena that form the center of the
analyses of Riesman, Kluckhohn, and others" consists merely of
"new *specifications* of the [unchanged] general value system, in
relation to new structural and situational conditions."[10]

It is of interest to juxtapose the studies of children's hero worship summarized in Table 7.1 with Lowenthal's findings on
changing heroes of popular biography and to discuss them in the
context of both Lowenthal's and Riesman's interpretations of the
former's findings. Lowenthal's conclusion that "idols of consumption" had taken the place of "idols of production" was based on
rather striking differences in the occupations of magazine biography subjects before and after World War I. Three major changes
were found in "the professional distribution of . . . 'heroes' "—
changes which Riesman saw as fitting snugly into the conclusions
of *The Lonely Crowd:*

1. Perhaps the most clear-cut change followed close upon the
growth, in the second decade of the century, of spectator sports

8. Richard deCharms and Gerald H. Moeller, "Values Expressed in American Children's Readers: 1800–1950," *Journal of Abnormal and Social Psychology*, 64 (1962), 136–42.

9. Seymour M. Lipset, "A Changing American Character?" in Lipset and
Lowenthal, p. 140.

10. Talcott Parsons and Winston White, "The Link between Character and
Society," ibid., p. 103. Also see Winston White, *Beyond Conformity* (New
York, The Free Press of Glencoe, 1961).

and the mass entertainment industry. During the period before the first World War, 77 per cent of the biographies of entertainers were of representatives of "serious arts" (i.e. literature, fine arts, music, dance, theatre). For each successive time period sampled there was a consistent shift in the direction of representatives of athletics and of what Lowenthal refers to as "the sphere of cheap or mass entertainment," until by 1940–41 "serious artists" made up only nine per cent of the entertainers about whom biographies were written. Overall, biographies of entertainers ("serious" and "non-serious") accounted for only a fourth of the pre-World War I biographies as opposed to one half of the postwar biographies. Lowenthal concluded that "the [contemporary] idols of the masses are not, as they were in the past, the leading names in the battle of production, but the headliners of the movies, the ballparks, and the night clubs."[11]

2. The overall decline in biographies of leaders "in the battle of production" was not as sharp as the increase in biographies of entertainers. Leaders of production made up 28 per cent of the pre-1914 biographies and an average of about 17 per cent of the biographies in the three later time periods sampled by Lowenthal. But here also the differences were greater if one took account of the degree to which the biographical subjects represented the "serious side" of life. Early biographies were of bankers and railroad executives; the later ones concentrated on such figures as the owner of a vacation resort, a man who had organized a roadside restaurant chain, and a professional model.

3. Finally, consistent with the assertion in *The Lonely Crowd* that, with the advent of other-direction, politics increasingly has become a passive spectator activity rather than an arena in which

11. Lowenthal, "Biographies in Popular Magazines," p. 517. In a brief aside, Lowenthal raises the possibility that the subjects of magazine biographies were representative merely of the "ideology" of the time, ibid., p. 513. Riesman, however, seems to assume that they represent attitudes in the general population. ("Surveys of content in the mass media show a shift in the kinds of information about business and political leaders that audiences ask for." *The Lonely Crowd*, p. 237.)

to vent intense feelings, biographies of political leaders were less common after World War I. Forty-six per cent of the early biographies were of people in political life; less than 30 per cent of the later biographies were of politicians.

Both Lowenthal and Riesman interpret the shifts in biographical heroes since the turn of the century in terms of a decline in popular aspiration levels. Biographies during the early period were "to be looked upon as examples of success which can be imitated," Lowenthal suggests. Taking note of the rhetoric in the biographies as well as the individuals who were their subjects, he concludes that during the early period such magazine articles served as "educational models." They reflected a period of "rugged individualism . . . characterized by eagerness and confidence that the social ladder may be scaled on a mass basis." The later biographies, on the other hand, "seem to lead to a dream world of the masses who no longer are capable or willing to conceive of biographies primarily as a means of orientation and education."[12]

Riesman agrees that biographies during the early period served as models which were within the aspirations of their readers, whereas today the individual "cannot imagine himself in the work role of the president of the United States or the head of a big company." However, he suggests that the contemporary biographies also are models; but these are new, other-directed models of taste, life-style, and leisure-time pursuit—"the frontiers on which the reader can himself compete."[13]

Besides using the data on trends in children's exemplars to determine whether Lowenthal's content analysis findings are valid indicators of changes in "the idols of the masses," they may also be used to establish whether one other shift in the type of exemplar chosen by children, which might be anticipated from speculations in *The Lonely Crowd*, has taken place. Riesman suggests that identification with national heroes served an important function in the socialization of children during the period when society was "dependent on inner direction."

12. Lowenthal, p. 517.
13. *The Lonely Crowd*, p. 273.

> [In] the George Washington myth . . . not only are the
> little boys told in the period of inner direction that they may
> grow up to be president but they are given scales by which
> to measure and discipline themselves for the job during boy-
> hood. If they do not tell lies, if they work hard, and so on—
> if, that is, they act in their boyhoods as the legendary Wash-
> ington acted in his—then they may succeed to his adult
> role.[14]

Although Riesman does not explicitly state that the use of national heroes as childhood models has declined over the years,
this conclusion is consistent with his discussion.

TRENDS IN CHILDREN'S HEROES SINCE THE
TURN OF THE CENTURY

In addition to drawing on the five studies (summarized in
Table 7.1) which were suitable for retabulation, the following
analysis makes impressionistic use of other internal evidence from
the studies, including lengthy but not exhaustive inventories of
children's statements about why they chose to be like their hero,
and additional studies which did not supply sufficiently comparable
or detailed data for retabulation. We shall be concerned with
(1) whether the direct questionnaire data confirm the trends in
"hero worship" suggested by Lowenthal's indirect data, and (2)
more fundamentally, whether the pattern of findings in the
various direct studies of children is consistent with the belief that
popular aspiration levels have declined.

1. *Entertainers:* Following Lowenthal, I have defined "entertainer" in the broadest sense of the word to encompass not only
popular performers such as film stars and professional athletes,
but also all representatives of literature and the arts. Included are
figures from the past (e.g. Longfellow and even Mozart) as well
as those who were living at the times of the various studies.

The long-run trends in children's responses are generally con-

14. Ibid., p. 96.

TABLE 7.1. Choices by Children and Adolescents of Various Classes of
Public Figures as Exemplars: 1902–1958[a]

	Place, Approximate Date of Field Work, and Investigator				
	1902	1910	1928	1944	1958
Exemplars	New Castle, Pa. Chambers	Nashville, Tenn. Hill	Birmingham, Montgomery, Mobile, Ala. Hill	Springfield, Mass. Stoughton, Ray	New Haven, Conn. Greenstein
Entertainment					
"Serious"	4.1%	4.1%	5.1%	—	1.8%
"Non-Serious"	.6	.3	10.4	8.1%	36.1
Business	1.6	1.0	1.0	—	.6
Contemporary political					
Incumbent president	3.3	.9	.2	2.7	3.3
Other	9.2	1.4	2.2	.4	3.0
National hero					
Washington	29.2	22.0	19.9	4.9	3.2
Lincoln	3.4	.6	2.4	1.5	3.6
Other	3.0	9.6	5.1	4.6	3.6
Miscellaneous figures from wider environment	17.2	20.6	15.6	33.4	14.8
Immediate environment figures	22.4	39.5	33.8	44.4	2.0
No response or invalid response	6.0	—	4.3	—	28.0
Total	100.0	100.0	100.0	100.0	100.0
Ages included in present tabulation	7–16	7–15	6–20	9&11	9–15
Number of cases	2333	1431	8813	259	659

a. Further information about the five studies summarized here, along with a discussion of the technique of retabulation and estimation, is contained in Appendix C. A number of the percentages in the table are estimates of the percentages which would have resulted if certain minor gaps in the data did not exist. All estimates are between a fraction of one per cent and about three per cent of what would have been found if full data were available, with the exception of the 1902 statistic for "other national heroes," which is—to some unknown degree—larger than the three per cent indicated in the table. In each case where an estimate has been made the estimate is conservative with respect to the interpretation of the table in the text, so that any other estimate would have further strengthened the conclusions. (For example, the highest possible estimate is used for "other contemporary political figures" in 1902, and the lowest possible estimate in 1944.) The "miscellaneous figures from wider environment" category is residual. It includes, among others, scientists, inventors, military leaders, religious figures, and characters from fiction, as well as a small number of responses which could not be classified because the names of the exemplars were not listed or were unidentifiable.

Invalid responses (e.g. references to an occupation rather than an individual, illegible questionnaires, etc.) were eliminated from the 1910 study prior to analysis. These made up about three per cent of the original 1910 sample. There is no discussion of invalid responses or of failures to respond in the 1944 study, and none are reported. The 1944 study was of second grade (age 7), fourth grade (age 9), and sixth grade (age 11) children; I have retabulated the percentages, eliminating the second grade subsample in order to bring the mean age closer to that of the other studies. Even after retabulation the mean age of this sample is still somewhat lower than that of the other samples. This evidently accounts for the greater tendency of 1944 respondents to refer to immediate environment exemplars. The size of the residual "miscellaneous" category in this study is a function partly of wartime references to military heroes and partly of a somewhat larger number of unidentified exemplars. See Appendix C for a fuller discussion.

The data in this table also may be presented with the percentages computed only on the basis of references to wider environment exemplars in order to eliminate the variability in response and in reference to immediate environment exemplars. This organization of the data would affect none of the results discussed below.

sistent with Lowenthal's findings. In particular, the change he observed in the ratio of "serious" and "non-serious" artists is clearly evident. Before World War I both the percentages in Table 7.1 and the authors' discussions of their findings indicate that children rarely referred to popular performers. By 1928, the proportion of popular figures referred to (e.g. Clara Bow, Rudolph Valentino, Ty Cobb, Paul Whiteman) is double that of "serious" artists; in the post-1944 samples, references to the latter category virtually disappear.[15] Because the decline of "serious artists" is

15. Evidently none of the 1944 children referred to "serious" artists. The findings of Havighurst et al., although presented in categories which are not strictly comparable to the present ones, provide supporting evidence that children have tended to choose popular entertainers as their exemplars in recent decades. Their study, which was of nine different populations of children and adolescents—most of them Midwesterners—seems to have been conducted

accompanied by an increase in "non-serious" artists, and because of the possibility that the phrasing of the 1958 item "increased" the frequency of reference to entertainers, it is not certain whether overall references to entertainers have increased.

2. *Businessmen, industrialists, financiers:* Lowenthal's procedure was to combine business and professional occupations into a single category, the latter including such disparate types as a college president and an inventor of gadgets. Then he further analyzed the occupations in terms of whether they were "serious" or "non-serious" and whether they represented production or consumption spheres of life.

In Table 7.1, I have reported only the proportion of references to "captains of industry" (industrialists, financiers, and businessmen in general). This avoids a great many troublesome coding decisions about whether a profession is "serious" and at the same time provides a clear-cut test of whether veneration of "idols of production" has declined.

The findings summarized in Table 7.1 cast serious doubt on the assumption that the frequent pre-World War I magazine biographies of captains of industry were an accurate indication of mass aspirations at the time. If such goals were prevalent in the population, it is difficult to believe that they would not have been reflected in children's statements about who they would "care to

---

in 1944 or 1945. The total number of respondents is 1,147. Havighurst et al. present a category of exemplars labeled "glamorous adults," including "people with a romantic or ephemeral fame, due to the more superficial qualities of appearance and behavior—e.g. movie stars, military figures, athletes," as well as "characters in comic strips or radio dramas." Their discussion suggests that most of the references coded in this category were to popular entertainers. In three of the populations they studied, references to "glamorous adults" exceeded 30 per cent and in four they exceeded 20 per cent. In the remaining two the percentages were 14 and 2. The item used in this study permitted references both to individuals personally known by the respondents and to imaginary "composite characters," as well as to public figures. The inclusion of the "composite" category (numerous responses were classified under this heading) presumably reduces references to figures in the wider environment and therefore makes Havighurst's estimate of the frequency of "glamorous" exemplars conservative.

be like or resemble." But only a minute proportion (less than two per cent) of the children in the early studies referred to men like Carnegie, Rockefeller, and Morgan as their "ideals." It is true that still fewer contemporary children make such choices (none seem to have in the 1944 study). But the decline is within an exceedingly small range.

3. *Contemporary political figures:* The incumbent president and other living politicians have been placed in this category, plus individuals who were active during the adult lifetimes of parents of the children studied. Thus for the 1958 respondents, Franklin D. Roosevelt is treated as "contemporary"; Woodrow Wilson and Theodore Roosevelt have the same status for the 1928 children.

The data on contemporary political figures also cast doubt on the adequacy of Lowenthal's index. During all periods very few children chose the incumbent president. The proportion of 1902 references to Theodore Roosevelt, for example, is virtually identical with the proportion of 1944 references to Franklin Roosevelt, and in general there is no significant variation over the half century in references to the chief executive. Studies of children's occupational goals conducted around the turn of the century further support the finding that children of that period rarely developed presidential aspirations.[16]

16. If log cabin-to-White House mythology ever had much of an impact on children's aspirations, it must have been in the period before the 1890s, judging from the several studies of children's occupational preferences published around the turn of the century. For example, in a study of the responses of 1,065 five- through sixteen-year-old Brooklyn, New York, Long Branch, New Jersey, and Melrose, Massachusetts, children to the question, "What would you like to be when you grow up?" only 11 references to the presidency emerged. Adelaide E. Wyckoff, "Children's Ideals," *The Pedagogical Seminary*, 8 (December 1901), 482–92. In another early study (the field work took place in 1893) 1,234 Santa Rosa and San Jose, California, public school children were read an anecdote describing a group of children expressing their occupational preferences. Included in the occupations listed was president. Some children made this choice, but apparently too few to be included in a table which lists occupations referred to as infrequently as six times. Hatti M. Willard, "Children's Ambitions," *Studies in Education*, 1 (January 1897), 243–53. The discussions of two other early studies, neither of which presents tabulations, also

At first glance there seems to be partial support for Lowenthal's thesis in the finding that "other contemporary political figures" were chosen by about nine per cent of the 1902 respondents, in contrast to three per cent or less of the respondents in later studies. But two thirds of the "other" 1902 references were to the recently assassinated President McKinley and there is evidence that during the period immediately after his death, McKinley's "martyrdom" led to a widespread idolization of him on the part of children, as well as adults.[17]

4. *National heroes:* Riesman's discussion of the erstwhile role of national heroes in children's socialization leads us to expect that references to the *dramatis personae* of American patriotic lore will have declined. And this indeed is the case. Over 35 per cent of the 1902 responses and only about 10 per cent of the post-1944 responses fell in this category. In the first of the reports on children's exemplars—Darrah's 1896 study of 1,440 St. Paul, Minnesota, and San Mateo County, California, children[18]—references to Washington and Lincoln alone (by far the most frequent-

---

suggest that when children in the 1890s were asked "What would you like to be?" few of them mentioned the presidency. Will S. Monroe, "Vocational Interests of Children," *Education, 18* (January 1898), 259–64, a study of 1,755 eight- to sixteen-year-old school children from a number of Connecticut River Valley communities in Massachusetts; and J. P. Taylor, "A Preliminary Study of Children's Hopes," *Forty-Second Annual Report of the State Superintendent for the School Year Ending July 31, 1895,* State of New York Department of Public Instruction, *2,* 987–1015, a study of 2,000 school children from various New York State communities. These occupational preference studies present extensive quotations of children's responses and therefore are of considerable impressionistic interest. Unfortunately, they are not suitable for systematic secondary analysis.

17. A few weeks after McKinley's assassination, Earl Barnes asked 1,800 seven- through seventeen-year-old Long Branch, New Jersey, and Winfield, New York, children to write essays on the topic, "Would you wish to be like Mr. McKinley? Why?" Ninety-two per cent of the responses were positive and the remaining eight per cent apparently consisted not of personal rejections of McKinley, but rather of statements such as "I would not like to have the care he had on his mind all the time." Earl Barnes, "Political Ideas of American Children," *Studies in Education, 2* (1902), 25–30.

18. Darrah, p. 94.

ly mentioned patriotic figures in all of the studies) were made by 40 per cent of the ten- to sixteen-year-old respondents. The breakdown of national heroes reported in Table 7.1 leads to a further observation: one name—George Washington—seems to account for the entire declining trend in references to national heroes.

To recapitulate, the direct data on children's exemplars are consistent with only one of the three trends reported by Lowenthal. The ratio of popular over serious entertainers has increased over the years in roughly the same way that the content of magazine biographies has shifted. But changes in magazine biographies of "heroes of production" and of political leaders are not reflected in children's reports of their exemplars. The direct data also support Riesman's hypothesis that contemporary children are less likely than their predecessors to identify with national heroes. We may now consider the implications of these findings.

HAS THE SOCIALIZATION OF ACHIEVEMENT ASPIRATION DECLINED?

In general, the body of "forgotten" data discussed here provides little if any support for the notion that Americans have placed a declining value on achievement. It is true that when one compares official emanations (for example, addresses to high school and college graduating classes) of the past with those of today "the decline of the Protestant ethic" seems plentifully evident. But this comparison may merely confound *fin de siècle* rationalizations with reality. DeCharms and Moeller find that between 1880 and 1910 "achievement imagery" in children's textbooks was about twice as common as it is in the contemporary period. This, they imply, indicates that achievement values were more prevalent then than now, a factor which they feel helps to explain industrial growth during those years.[19] Yet, in view of the consistently low rate of choice of businessmen as exemplars, it is difficult to believe that turn-of-the-century young people surpassed contemporary youths in the desire to excel in economic enterprise.

19. deCharms and Moeller, pp. 141–42.

The absence of business exemplars is especially striking in the face of what, on Lowenthal's showing, seems to have been a concerted attempt in the media to display businessmen as models for popular emulation.

Similarly, rhetoric suggesting that "every boy is a potential President of the United States" abounded 60 years ago. Consider, for example, the statement by the author of one of the early studies that this "feeling . . . is one of our prized possessions. Our school literature is full of it; no address before children is complete which fails to remind them that each is on his way to the presidential chair."[20] As we have seen, the rhetoric seems to have had little impact on children's felt aspirations—choice of the incumbent president as an exemplar was exceedingly rare.

The two classes of exemplar which *did* shift over the half century—entertainers and national heroes—are quite ambiguous indicators of aspiration levels. There is no a priori reason for assuming that the individual who wanted to be like Enrico Caruso or Jenny Lind was more driven to succeed than someone who sets up Frank Sinatra or Debbie Reynolds as an ideal. The reverse could as easily be true. The decline in reference to national heroes (or, more precisely, references to Washington) is equally difficult to interpret. One hypothesis, which at first seems credible, is that identification with a hero such as Washington serves to channel a child's aspirations in the direction of political achievement. This seems to have been Riesman's assumption in the passage quoted above about the function of the George Washington myth in the period "dependent upon inner direction." His remarks continue:

> The [presidential] role, moreover, by its very nature, is a continuing one; somebody is always president . . . In fantasy the little boy not only identifies with the young Washington in the French and Indian wars but also with the adult role of president.[21]

If this were the case, we would expect—contrary to the present findings—that populations high in identification with figures like

20. Barnes, "Political Ideas of American Children," p. 28.
21. *The Lonely Crowd*, p. 96.

Washington also would be high in reference to incumbent presidents.

Unfortunately, respondents' explanations of why they chose to be like their exemplars were not presented exhaustively in the early studies. Therefore they cannot be retabulated. However, the extensive quotations that are given also fail to support the Riesmanian conception of an era in which the socialization process instilled in children lofty aspirations—*ad astra per aspera*.[22] The responses reported in the early studies are not couched in the language of personal striving, nor do they carry the implication that the child expected personally to assume the role of the individual to whom he referred. The largest proportion of statements seem simply to ascribe to the child's hero what one of the early writers called "rather vague moral qualities."[23] ("I want to be like George Washington because he was good.") Other responses stress the fame of the child's exemplar, his wealth (but without the implication that by emulating his hero the child expects personally to obtain riches), his physical appearance.

Even the first of the studies (1896) contains quotations which, with slight alterations in prose style, might have served as epigraphs for chapters in *The Lonely Crowd* on the other-directed way of life. For example, a fifteen-year-old boy explained shortly before the election of 1896 that he wanted to be like William Jennings Bryan because Bryan "is well proportioned and well built, a good looking gentleman, and one of the smartest men in the United States . . . and is, without an exception, the greatest orator on the face of the globe." In the same study, a fourteen-year-old boy selected as his idol a man he wanted to resemble "because he has not very hard work, and he has a good time and plenty of money."[24]

The assumption that achievement values have changed may, as Lipset's remarks suggest, simply be the result of inaccurate con-

22. Ibid., pp. 118–20.

23. Barnes, p. 28.

24. Darrah, pp. 90–92. Similar statements may be found in the numerous quotations of children's reasons for preferring occupations reported in the studies cited in note 16.

ceptions of nineteenth-century America. Writers who emphasize
the passivity of contemporary Americans usually at least tacitly
picture a much more vigorous, optimistic, upwardly striving folk
who populated what Lowenthal calls the "open-minded liberal
society" at the beginning of the century.[25] But commentators on
the present often find it tempting to idealize the past.[26] Certain
mistaken notions about structural changes in American society
in the present century probably have contributed to the commonly
held belief that American aspiration levels have declined. For
example, until recently it was widely assumed that upward occupational mobility has diminished in the United States. This assumption has been severely challenged by recent research.[27] Similarly,
questionable assertions about the debilitating effects of contemporary "mass society" may have predisposed observers to accept over-
simplified, if not erroneous, hypotheses about value change.[28]

25. It is interesting to compare Lowenthal's characterization of turn-of-the-
century American society with the following observation by one of the early
students of children's occupational preferences: "The small number of extrava-
gant impossible hopings [among the respondents] seems quite remarkable. The
apparent contentment with the lot nature has given them, the genuine delight
with which the poorer children look forward to the severe monotonous labors
that the future holds in store, the glad willingness to share the heavy burdens
of supporting their father's family, all are witnesses to the triumph of childhood's hope and idealism over the toil and pain of the world." Taylor, p. 999.
Children during this period doubtless were not devoid of mobility aspirations.
Cf. Monroe's comparisons of Massachusetts children's occupational preferences
with parental occupations, which suggest, for example, that children of unskilled laborers often aspired toward skilled trades.

26. For one likely intellectual source of such idealizations see Richard
Hofstadter, *Social Darwinism in American Thought: 1860–1915* (Philadel-
phia, University of Pennsylvania Press, 1944). Cf. also, R. Richard Wohl, "The
'Rags to Riches Story': An Episode of Secular Idealism," in Bendix and Lipset,
Class, Status and Power, pp. 388–95.

27. Natalie Rogoff, *Recent Trends in Occupational Mobility* (Glencoe, Ill.,
The Free Press, 1953); Seymour M. Lipset and Reinhard Bendix, *Social
Mobility in Industrial Society* (Berkeley, University of California Press, 1959).

28. Cf., for example, Daniel Bell, "America as a Mass Society: A Critique,"
Commentary, 32 (July 1956), 75–83; Scott Greer and Peter Orleans, "Mass
Society and Parapolitical Structure," *American Sociological Review,* 27 (1962),
634–46.

CAUSES AND CONSEQUENCES OF
CHANGING EXEMPLARS

I have been at pains to suggest that, contrary to much contemporary speculation, *one* aspect of children's learning has remained stable: there is no evidence that achievement aspirations have gone down since the turn of the century. But this is not to say that all of the values transmitted in the socialization process have been static.

At the very least, we have the clear evidence in Table 7.1 of two concrete and striking shifts in the ways children link themselves to the wider world—the sharp decline in references to patriotic figures as exemplars and the increase in references to popular entertainers. Furthermore, it is reasonable to believe that the values acquired by children have changed in other respects not connected with their choices of exemplars.

What has accounted for the two changes shown in Table 7.1? What is the broader significance of these changes? While we may speculate about the reasons for the changes with a certain degree of confidence, their positive significance is a good bit less evident.

The immediate causes of increased choice of popular entertainers would seem quite obviously to lie in the enormously greater availability of these figures for identification, resulting from the rise of a mass entertainment industry and new technologies of communication. The increase in the 1920s 'in references to popular entertainers directly parallels the growth of the motion picture industry and of radio. If the further increase between the 1944 and 1958 findings is not merely a function of the wording of the question used in the latter study, this also most probably has roots in technological change—the advent of television.[29]

At the turn of the century not only were there fewer popular entertainers who might serve as models for children; because of

29. By the date of the New Haven study, possession of a family television set evidently was close to universal. Only a handful of children reported that their family had no television set; interestingly, *none* of these children were from the lower socioeconomic status subsample.

the limited exposure allowed by personal appearances, there also was much less opportunity to see even the available entertainers. And entertainers were considered far less respectable and worthy of emulation than they are today (a point I shall return to).

The period we are considering, beginning with the turn of the century, saw still another complex of institutional changes relevant to changing exemplars—changes in school curriculum as part of the general "progressive education" movement. While it would be out of place here to attempt to characterize in detail "the transformation of the schools" during these years, we may note that one change has been the replacement of the traditional teaching of history with the broader and vaguer subject of "social studies."[30] Contemporary children undoubtedly are simply less often exposed to George Washington than were their predecessors.

There also may be something about the process of adopting public figures as exemplars that makes children's choices of them more changeable from generation to generation than are, say, party identifications. The early studies of children's exemplars, as I have pointed out, permitted choice of figures from both the immediate and the wider environment. Several of these studies report the frequency of both types of reference by age. Young children typically refer to parents, peers, and other individuals with whom they are personally acquainted. It is not until the child is nine or ten years of age that models from the wider environment are typically chosen. And it seems likely that these choices, unlike partisan preferences, for example, are influenced not by the parents but by reading, schoolteachers, the mass media, and other nonfamilial sources. In view of our discussion in Chapter 4 of the stability of *early* learning, the fact that the wider environment exemplar is acquired at a relatively *late* age may help to explain its mutability.[31]

30. See, for example, Wilhelmina Hill, *Social Studies in the Elementary School Program* (Washington, Department of Health, Education, and Welfare, 1960), p. 24, and Lawrence A. Cremin, *The Transformation of the School* (New York, Knopf, 1962).

31. Hill, "Comparative Study of Children's Ideals," p. 220; Hill, "Personification of Ideals by Urban Children," p. 382. Roger Masters has pointed out

What are we to make of the finding that children once looked to national heroes as their models and that today they admire Hollywood celebrities? To many the implications of national decay, of declining patriotism and civic responsibility, would seem obvious. Are they?

The brunt of my analysis of the Riesman thesis is to raise doubts about precisely this kind of facile generalization. What we need—and what this body of trend data unfortunately provides only in a fragmentary and impressionistic fashion—is evidence of the meaning to the child of choosing one or another kind of exemplar. Riesman, we have seen, assumed that a child taking George Washington as a hero would also come to think of the presidency as a meaningful life goal. But the available evidence suggests this was not the case. It also might be argued that declining identification with national heroes inevitably would lead to declining national loyalty. While I have no data on trends in national loyalty, it was quite clear that the New Haven children were intense national partisans. American defeats and achievements in space satellite competition, for example, were observed with the utmost interest and responded to with high feelings.

We cannot assume that the tendency of children of several generations ago to choose Washington as a hero was in some way an automatic sign of their greater civic virtue. In fact, contemporary accounts deplored the shallowness and superficiality of teaching about American heroes, and, perhaps in anticipation of later educational trends, we find explicit statements in the early studies urging that less attention be paid in the grammar schools to George Washington hagiolatry.[32]

If identification with Washington was not necessarily a sign of virtue, the references of today's children to entertainers are not necessarily indices of some sort of degeneration. Kluckhohn has

---

to me that in Plato's classic analysis of political change resulting from what in effect is "defective" socialization (*The Republic,* viii and ix), change takes place when the normal agent of socialization (the father) is replaced by some other agent such as servants, or the mother.

32. For example, Chambers.

suggested a number of interesting refinements of the theses of
declining aspiration levels and increasing "other-directedness."
His hypotheses may help further to explain the increasing references to popular entertainers as exemplars.

Contemporary American youths, he argues, unlike previous
generations, are conspicuous for their "hedonistic and present-
time valuation."

> I do not, however, employ "hedonism" in its pejorative
> sense, for it strikes me that there is considerably less hedon-
> ism of this sort than there was in the decade after World
> War I. I mean, rather, the value which Puritanism never
> placed upon recreation (except as a means to the end of more
> effective work), pleasure, leisure, and aesthetic and expres-
> sive activities. Americans enjoy themselves more and with
> less guilt than ever before.[33]

Kluckhohn argues, in effect, that there have been fundamental
changes in the outlook of the current (post-World War II)
generation of Americans, but that these are not simply changes in
the direction of conformity and passivity. Young Americans have
moved in the direction of an "outward conformity of behavior,"
but this has not been accompanied by "an inward conformity of
thought and feeling." "Today's kind of conformity," he suggests,
"may actually be a step toward more genuine individuality in the
United States."

> I sense that in the younger generation conformity is less of
> a personal and psychological problem, less tinged with
> anxiety and guilt. If one accepts outwardly the conventions
> of the face-to-face group, one may have greater psychic
> energies to develop and fulfill one's private potentialities as
> a unique person.[34]

33. Clyde Kluckhohn, "Shifts in American Values," *World Politics*, 11
(1959), 257.
34. Ibid., p. 258.

Among other things, he suggests, Americans have lost interest in conspicuous consumption, they have become increasingly interested in matters of psychology and mental health, and they have come to be less automatically chauvinistic and more likely to prize diversity in values and life styles.[35]

The increasing tendency to choose entertainers as exemplars could well be a part of the trends described by Kluckhohn: The "obvious" interpretation in terms of mass passivity and irresponsibility turns out on close examination not to be obviously valid. In fact there is at the moment no fully satisfactory way to interpret the significance of these findings of changes in children's learning. The data simply are insufficient for more than the most tendentious hypothesizing. The significance of children's choices of exemplars becomes fully clear only when we have reasonably comprehensive data on the meaning of the choice to the child. The same choice may have different meanings in different historical periods, and different meanings to different children during the same period. Therefore, it is necessary to have data not only on choice of exemplar, but also on the meaning to the child of his choice. Eventually, it also will be important to have a reliable understanding of the significance of his early heroes and hero worship for the child's later development.

Thus, although our attempt to indicate the positive significance of the present body of data is unsatisfactory, certain methodological points become clear. It evidently is important to develop trend data in richer detail than has been the case. We need not only inventories of responses, but also knowledge of the meanings of responses. In addition, these findings suggest that we need richer and more detailed theories to guide research and analysis. One of the difficulties here is that little has been written explicitly

35. Ibid., p. 259. As can be seen simply from the frequency of references to George Washington in Table 7.1, a great many children made the *same* choice of exemplar in the earlier of the studies discussed here. In New Haven, in 1958, no public figure was chosen by more than four per cent of the sample; of the 55 entertainment and 18 sports figures referred to, none was mentioned by more than three per cent of the sample.

dealing at the theoretical level with the kind of response we are discussing. The categories of "identification" and "ego ideal" exist in the psychological literature, but little has been written about identifications beyond the immediate environment, or about the developmental significance of selecting wider environment figures as ego-ideals.[36] And the research on these problems is essentially nonexistent. Thus the problems arising from our applied analysis of psychological development may suggest a number of tasks which might usefully become part of the agenda of basic research.

This methodological conclusion provides us with a logical transition to discussion of avenues of further inquiry in political socialization.

36. See the references to the literature on identification in note 21, Chapter 4. The various discussions in the psychoanalytic literature of the functions of the ego-ideal also fail to shed much light on the frequency with which public figures fulfill this function and the significance of choice of public figures as ego-ideals. See, for example, Samuel Novey, "The Role of the Superego and Ego-Ideal in Character Formation," *International Journal of Psychoanalysis*, 36 (1955), 254–59.

CHAPTER 8

Avenues for Further Inquiry

"The analysis of . . . political socialization in a particular society," as Almond comments,

> is basic to the whole field of political analysis, since it not
> only gives us insight into the pattern of political culture and
> subcultures in that society, but also locates for us in the social-
> ization processes of the society the points where particular
> qualities and elements of the political culture are introduced,
> and the points in the society where these elements are being
> sustained or modified.[1]

In this study it has been possible to consider only a handful of the many aspects of political socialization that deserve inquiry. And we have examined only a single sample of fourth through eighth grade children, in one community and one culture at one point in time.

I now turn briefly to the implications of the New Haven find-ings and, more generally, to a consideration of the tactics of in-quiry which might be fruitful in studying political socialization. The next step might be the specification of hypotheses for research, but, since virtually every aspect of adult political behavior can be studied in terms of its pre-adult antecedents, the universe of

1. Gabriel A. Almond, "A Functional Approach to Comparative Politics," in *The Politics of the Developing Areas*, p. 31.

possible hypotheses is simply too large to consider here. Furthermore, it is an ever-expanding universe.

IMPLICATIONS OF THE NEW HAVEN FINDINGS

Résumé of the findings

We have taken note of children's feelings toward political
authority, the development of their political information and
partisan motivations, the relationship between social class and
political learning, sex differences in political learning, and change
and continuity over the years in children's exemplars. Without
attempting to be exhaustive, we may review certain of the main
conclusions.

The child's first conception of political authority seems to have
more *affective* than cognitive content. The child, like the adult,
has a quite firm impression that figures such as the President of
the United States are important, but he has no clear understanding
of what these individuals do. The affective response to political
leaders is strikingly *positive,* more so than adult responses to
leaders. Children's feelings toward politicians are unambivalent.
The prevailing adult theme of cynicism toward politics and politicians evidently develops at adolescence or later.

The precedence of affective over cognitive learning also is apparent in the development of partisan motivations, especially
party identification. Children acquire party attachments before
they can make more than the most fragmentary distinctions about
the nature of political parties, about what the parties stand for,
even about who the parties' public representatives are. Party
preferences are fixed early; they precede the advent of issue
orientations, or "mature" evaluations of candidates. Thus, from
an early age, party preferences are available for shaping issue and
candidate preferences and, more generally, for perceiving the
world of politics.

Information about political institutions begins with awareness
of the names of a few conspicuous public officials—the president,

and in New Haven, the mayor. Gradually an awareness of their duties develops. At each level of government, it is the *executive* who is understood before the legislative body and the individual legislators. Among the levels of government, the *federal* is the first at which there is awareness of both executive and legislature; the state level is the last about which learning takes place.

The *leitmotif* of our analysis of political development was the importance of early learning. Children seem first to become familiar with and adopt the orientations which are important in the behavior of adults: party rather than issue or candidate orientations; information about the national and local political arenas, rather than the state level, and about executives rather than legislatures. In addition, the positive side of adult orientations toward political leaders is learned before attitudes of political cynicism are adopted; and these positive orientations seem to have more bearing on adult political behavior than do the negative orientations.

In part, political orientations which are important to adults are first learned by children because these are the orientations adults are most likely to display before children and to be able to explain to children. Orientations learned at an early age also may have reciprocal effects on adult attitudes because early learning occurs during a plastic, formative period, and can affect later learning.

Differences in the political participation of adults of different social class backgrounds and of men and women are clearly presaged by similar differences among preadolescent children. In both cases, the *pattern* of childhood political differences, and the more general pattern of *nonpolitical* socialization differences, help us to understand the adult phenomenon.

Lower-status child-rearing practices foster compliance to authority; upper-status socialization places a much greater emphasis on self-expression and individual aspiration. And we find that upper-status children are a good bit more capable than lower-status children of criticizing political authority and more readily learn to perceive themselves as independent judges of political events. In addition, of course, lower-status children acquire from their parents less political information and fewer incentives to participate in politics than do upper-status children. They also are less likely to develop the sorts of skills that facilitate political action and communication.

From an early age girls show less political interest and awareness than boys, even though girls are better able to manipulate language than boys and are, by many psychosocial standards, more "grown-up" than boys. Here the crucial factor evidently is the early sex-typing of interests, especially nonpolitical interests. Through processes such as identification with the parent of the same sex, rewards and punishments for sex-appropriate activities, and play and fantasy activities, sex roles are learned early in life. Among other things, the sexes acquire substantially different interests—girls are attentive to the home, the local community, and to their immediate environment; boys acquire much more far-flung interests and aspirations. Sex differences in aggressiveness also may have something to do with the greater political involvement of young boys. Gradually children acquire an explicit conception of politics as a male function.

In Chapter 7, which was based upon a half century of studies of children's exemplars, we shifted our attention from learning that fosters continuity between the generations in political behavior to changes in children's learning. Since the turn of the century, children have become much less likely to choose patriotic heroes as exemplars and much more likely to select figures from the sphere of popular entertainment. During the same period, however, there has been little change in reference to contemporary politicians, such as the incumbent president, and to businessmen. A satisfactory interpretation of these changes is not possible, because too little is known about the personal significance of choices of public figures as exemplars. Nevertheless, both quantitative and qualitative evidence from this time series of studies serves the negative function of raising serious doubts about certain widespread theories of psychological change in the present century; *viz.* the theories which point to declining popular aspiration levels.

Implications for the political system

The scope of political analysis in the twentieth century has progressively widened. From exclusive preoccupation with the formal properties of government, scholars have broadened their concerns to encompass the informal realities of political life and the nongovernmental environment of politics. Attention has successively moved from the structure of government to its functioning; from government itself to political parties, interest groups, and observation of public opinion and electoral behavior. The present study contributes to this process of expansion by examining the childhood antecedents of adult political behavior.

Anything approaching a comprehensive analysis of the effects of political socialization on the political system would have to be based upon a far more extensive body of knowledge than presently exists. But the present findings at least make it clear that important aspects of adult political behavior have their roots in the early political learning of the child. And even with the limited New Haven sample and findings, it has been possible to suggest a few of the points at which the socialization process affects the political system.

In view of the emphasis in much contemporary writing on public conceptions of the legitimacy of existing institutions as a determinant of political stability, one striking finding of this study (and the related research by Easton and Hess) is the exceptionally favorable quality of children's earliest conceptions of American government and politics. Assumptions that political leaders are benign develop early in childhood. Almost imperceptibly, the rising generation of children comes to accept and place a favorable evaluation on the going political system. Children's attachments to the system are no less firm as a result of the declining importance of certain of the classic symbols of patriotism—for instance, the celebration of national heroes such as Washington. And it may well be because the child is insulated (and insulates himself) from the cynical side of adult political attitudes that the

latter seem in many ways to be merely skin deep—to have little
detrimental effect on the system.

I have stressed—perhaps to the point of tedium—another connection between the socialization process and the political system.
To a considerable extent, political socialization seems to be conservative in its effects. Socialization processes foster the status quo
through the perpetuation of class and sex differences in political
participation, continuity between the generations in party preferences, continuation (and perhaps even strengthening) of adult
assessments of the relative importance of political institutions.

It should be made clear, however, that the effects of political
socialization are not inevitably conservative—and that the conservative effects of socialization are not necessarily desirable. The
continuities encouraged by socialization *may* foster political stability; this seems to be the case in the United States. But, as is suggested by the discussion, later in this chapter, of political socialization in France, the socialization process also may contribute to
the perpetuation of political instability. In either case, it is of
course a matter of independent judgment whether socialization,
by encouraging continuity, is an obstacle to desirable change.

As the assertion by Almond quoted at the beginning of this
chapter suggests, the socialization process can be the point in the
social order at which existing patterns are *modified* rather than
sustained. Some change in political learning presumably results
from stimuli which affect all age levels in society more or less
equally. Change also can result from events (such as unemploy-
ment), which have their most immediate effect on the older
generation, but which influence children through the mediation
of parental instruction. As Inkeles points out, in a discussion of
the differences in child-raising in Russia before and after the
Revolution, socialization is future oriented—parents may inten-
tionally depart from traditional child-rearing practices in order
to prepare their offspring for the changing requirements of their
society.[2] Whether or not children are deliberately raised different-

2. Alex Inkeles, "Social Change and Social Character: The Role of Parental
Mediation," *Journal of Social Issues, 11* (1955), 12–23.

ly from their parents, any practices that contribute to differential experience between generations carry with them the seeds of change. In the United States, both vertical and horizontal social mobility have been found to encourage intergenerational political change, perhaps the most striking differences in experience being those between the first and later generations of immigrants.[3] Elsewhere in the world, especially in the developing areas, the differences in experience between generations may be even more radical. Consider the following autobiographical report of a young African, who began life as a Masai tribesman and received a Western education.

> When I go home on leave now I find it difficult to associate with youths of my age. They don't understand my putting on Western clothes. They cannot tolerate a half-Masai. All the same I understand their pride and I stick to them through thick and thin. When I go home I try to adjust myself to their way of thinking. It is also true that when I leave home and go back to school, I have to adjust my way of thinking. And so it ends that I am destined to be between two worlds, each of which has a hold on me. Will it always be so? I think it will be.[4]

Before turning to the specific research implications of the New Haven findings a further observation may be made—less about the effects than about the nature of the American political socialization process. Although important political learning takes place during the childhood years in the United States, the political socialization of American school children is a remarkably effortless affair. As I have noted, many of the most fundamental political orientations (such as party preferences and conceptions of the functions and value of various political institutions) are learned by Americans without deliberate instruction and without much

3. Hyman, *Political Socialization*, pp. 123–51.
4. Katharine T. Kinkead, "Something To Take Back Home," *The New Yorker*, 40 (May 23, 1964), 107.

conscious awareness on the part of the socialized that learning is taking place.

One reason for assuming that early learning is important for later behavior is that early learning often has an unintended, inadvertent character. As a result, what one learns early is likely to be taken for granted and accepted unquestioningly. Richard Rose points out that in Great Britain, a nation especially notable for the strength of citizen adherence to the existing order, political socialization is largely an unplanned endeavor.

> It would be a mistake to think of the many agencies of political socialization [in Great Britain] as consciously attempting political indoctrination. Instead, this process seems to take place as a by-product of other functions. It is intimately linked with the family, schooling, early friends, and experiences at work. The result may be a political outlook that appears illogical or uninformed when judged by a political philosopher. But it is also an outlook that is strongly held, stable, and regarded by individuals as natural, just because it is rooted so deeply in their whole experience of English life.[5]

On the other hand, in France there has been much self-conscious attention to the political content of public education—and there has been even more in the totalitarian nations. The political socialization process, like the functioning of a healthy body, evidently is rarely recognized except when its performance is in some way deficient.

Research implications of the New Haven study

A number of the research implications of the New Haven findings should be immediately evident. Most obviously, replication is necessary. As I have emphasized, the observations are distilled from an exploratory survey; they are, in general, not tests of hy-

5. Richard Rose, *Politics in England* (Boston, Little, Brown, 1964), pp. 81–82.

potheses which were explicitly formulated and incorporated into the design of the research. Therefore, what seem to be central observations may prove merely to be idiosyncrasies of New Haven children in 1958, or even of the specific populations of New Haven children which composed the sample. Not only is replication with new and more satisfactory samples desirable, but it also will be important to extend the sample to include younger and older respondents. Where possible it is desirable to make use of longitudinal procedures[6] and to obtain *independent* observations on the agents of socialization as well as the child. It also will be important to develop and validate new measures of various phenomena which have proved to be interesting (e.g. idealization of political authority), in order to determine the degree to which findings from the present study are artifacts of the research procedure.

In general, my interpretations of the findings reported in Chapters 3 through 7 provide the most fruitful source of research hypotheses. Wherever possible, I have discussed the New Haven findings in connection with aspects of adult political behavior which they seem to foreshadow. Then I have interpreted the New Haven findings speculatively in terms of why the developmental pattern takes place and of its significance for understanding the individual's later political behavior and, more broadly, the working of the political system.

For example, I hypothesize that responses to family authority shape the child's first responses to authority in the wider environment. Idealization of political leaders may be an extension of, or a reaction to, orientations to the child's parents. Perception of hierarchical relationships between political leaders may be reflections of experiences with hierarchy in the home. It quite clearly would be desirable to study such connections directly by examining how children respond to authority in both their primary and secondary environments.

The interpretations in Chapter 4 of how partisan motivations

6. For a fuller discussion of longitudinal research see below.

and political information develop also pose research possibilities. At one point, for example, I suggest that the inability of young children to think abstractly is a major restraint upon the development of issue or ideological orientations during early preadolescence. If this is so, attempts to foster ideological commitments on the part of fourth or fifth graders should be generally unsuccessful; the capacity to evaluate issues and to develop internally consistent patterns of evaluations should be positively correlated with measures of general ability to use abstractions. In addition, insight into my formulation about the importance of early learning can be obtained by experimental modification of elementary school curricula.

The analyses of class and sex differences in children's political development suggest further research possibilities. In each case I argue that certain nonpolitical aspects of socialization are important in determining differential political involvement. It therefore would be of interest to determine whether lower-class children whose socialization has been "deviant" in the sense of encouraging independence of thought and upwardly mobile aspirations are (controlling for the political involvement of their parents) more interested in politics than lower-class children whose socialization has been more typical for their group. A similar design can be conceived for studying sex differences: is the little girl who is encouraged to engage in nondomestic fantasy and play more likely to develop an interest in politics than the child who is exclusively preoccupied with dolls and "playing house"?

A discussion of the research implications of the findings on changing exemplars appears at the conclusion of Chapter 7. In this instance further theorizing, as well as further empirical work on the personal significance of exemplars, is clearly in order. There has been little careful speculation on what it means for a young person to select models from the wider environment as his heroes.

These are a few of the research implications of New Haven findings. There are doubtless others, including some that have not been evident to me, but these remarks should be sufficient to suggest the kinds of inquiry which may be desirable. We may now turn more generally to some of the possible tactics of political socialization research, a number of which I have already hinted at.

RESEARCH TACTICS FOR THE STUDY OF POLITICAL SOCIALIZATION

In Chapter 1 we saw that there is a good bit of substantive, if not semantic, agreement about the kinds of data needed for a "full-blown characterization of political socialization." At a minimum, we would want detailed understanding of (1) the social and psychological characteristics of the individuals socialized, (2) what they learn, (3) the agents of socialization, (4) the circumstances of socialization, and (5) the effects of the learning process. An immediate goal of research would be to relate early childhood political (and politically relevant) learning to later childhood experience and learning. A longer-run goal, and one which has only recently begun to be met in child development research, is to relate childhood experience to adult behavior. This suggests the first of a number of possible research tactics.

The desirability of longitudinal research

Strictly speaking, the New Haven study reports no direct evidence of the *development* of political behavior, in spite of my use of this term on a number of occasions. Like much other research that goes by the label "developmental," the study is cross-sectional. That is, it examines different groups of children at successive age levels and assumes that systematic variation from year to year is evidence of developmental change. An alternative and more satisfactory (but also more expensive and difficult) tactic is that of the longitudinal study. Studies which follow the same individuals over time are familiar to political scientists mainly in the form of interviews with panels of voters during election campaigns.[7]

7. For example, Bernard Berelson et al., *Voting*.

One of the shortcomings of cross-sectional research is that findings which seem to be evidence of developmental trends may merely be the result of sampling variation. If, for example, sixth grade New Haven children show more issue involvement than fifth grade children, this may merely be because the sixth grade subsample happened to include a disproportionate number of children capable of handling abstractions.[8] More important, cross-sectional research does not provide us with observations on the *individual* child. When we find that most fifth graders are aware of the president and his duties, but that it is not until seventh grade that Congress is commonly understood, we infer, correctly for *most* children, that the president is understood before Congress. But the aggregate findings probably conceal cases in which the opposite sequence has taken place. And, in general, cross-sectional research makes it impossible to observe directly the effects of early learning on later experience.

A good bit of longitudinal research has been reported by psychologists, but most of it covers relatively short time sequences.[9] Recently, however, data have begun to accumulate from several systematic longitudinal studies, which began observing children in their infancy and continued to obtain observations into the adult years. Most notable among these is the impressive report by Kagan and Moss, who studied 71 young adults, correlating independently gathered psychological data on the adults with ob-

8. This possibility is especially strong when, as in the present study, the respondents are drawn from populations of individuals some of whom have a fund of common experience. In the New Haven study, as I have noted, information about formal governmental institutions varied by classroom, evidently as a result of the assiduousness with which "social studies" and "current events" were dealt with by the teacher.

9. A bibliography of longitudinal studies has been assembled by A. A. Stone and Gloria C. Onqué, *Longitudinal Studies of Child Personality: Abstracts with Index* (Cambridge, Harvard University Press, 1959). For an ingenious approach to combining longitudinal and cross-sectional procedures see Harold D. Lasswell, "The Method of Interlapping Observations in the Study of Personality and Culture," *Journal of Abnormal and Social Psychology*, 32 (1937), 240–45.

servational data from infancy on.[10] While it is not possible to summarize the results of this exciting study here, we may note a few relevant findings:

1. Some psychological patterns are remarkably *stable* from infancy to adult life.
2. Some early experiences exercise a *"sleeper effect"*; they have no seeming effect on middle and later childhood behavior, but do affect adult behavior.
3. Some patterns of childhood response are extinguished or reversed in later years, but seem nevertheless to affect adult behavior at the unconscious level.

It would be extraordinarily useful to tie political socialization research to such ongoing longitudinal studies. To my knowledge, none of the existing studies has examined political development, but one fascinating possibility would be to study the political orientations of adults on whom longitudinal data are available, and to relate adult political responses to earlier nonpolitical developmental patterns.

The possibility of experimental research

The controlled experiment, which, as Kagan and Moss point out,

> is admittedly the most potent weapon in the scientist's arsenal, is only amenable to selected problems in psychology. Many aspects of personality development are not subject to experimental manipulation. Aggressive children can not be transferred to loving homes; mothers can not be told to adopt a pattern of reinforcements so that the psychologists can have an aesthetically pleasing design.[11]

10. Jerome Kagan and Howard A. Moss, *Birth to Maturity* (New York, Wiley, 1962).
11. Ibid., p. 4.

Under some circumstances experimental socialization research *is* possible, however. I have already suggested this possibility in connection with certain of the New Haven findings about the seeming effects of early learning. School curricula may be systematically varied in order to determine the effects of (say): teaching young children about legislatures or state level politics before they learn of executives and national and local political institutions; exposing them to discussions of political issues; trying in various ways to augment their interest in politics; and so forth. Efforts to use the curriculum as an instrument for increasing interest in politics have been unsuccessful among college students,[12] but this may be because much of an individual's orientation toward politics already has become fixed by late adolescence.

Placing research in the context of child development theory and research

At one point it was possible tentatively to suggest the relationship of a New Haven finding—the spurt in proposals for "political change" between fourth and fifth grades—to findings of Gesell and Piaget about development unrelated to politics during the same period. Aspects of nonpolitical development also seem to help explain political class and sex differences in childhood. In general, however, I have not been able to relate the New Haven findings to any of the various theories of child development.

This certainly results in part from failure to incorporate such theories into the design of the study. But it is not immediately evident how this might best be done. Unfortunately, the general theories of development which have been spun out by Freud, Piaget, Sullivan, and Erikson, for example, have received only limited empirical verification. And they are poorly correlated with the empirical norms of development reported by child psy-

12. Marvin Schick and Albert Somit, "The Failure to Teach Political Activity," *The American Behavioral Scientist,* 6 (January 1963), 5–8, and the references there cited.

chologists, as well as with what little is known about the genesis of political and social orientations.

As child development research itself becomes more theoretically oriented, it should become increasingly possible to conceive of political development in terms of the development of that often-referred-to entity, the whole child. The New Haven data make it clear that this is necessary, that political development does not occur in a vacuum. Indeed some orientations which are fundamental to the individual's later political behavior seem to arise as unnoticed ancillary offshoots of nonpolitical development. In one sense, political socialization research may be seen as an applied aspect of *basic* socialization research, but a form of applied research which can occasionally feed back on and enrich basic research.

Specifying the social and political context within which socialization occurs

The numerous studies of child-rearing in primitive societies inevitably stress the effects of community cultural traditions and practices on socialization. Yet child development research in the United States and other Western nations has often ignored the social context. In *political* socialization research it is especially important to take account of the setting in which learning takes place.

Political socialization undoubtedly varies from community to community. Learning is not the same where political parties are strong as it is where parties are weak, for example. In states where legislation designed to weaken political parties is in force we find weaker party identifications and a lower absolute level of party identification;[13] differences in strength of attachment to parties evidently exist even within cities—between precincts with weak and strong party organizations.[14] We also would expect political

13. Campbell et al., *The American Voter*, p. 270.
14. Daniel Katz and Samuel J. Eldersveld, "The Impact of Local Party Activity on the Electorate," *Public Opinion Quarterly*, 25 (1961), 19.

learning to vary, *inter alia,* between large and small communities, North and South, areas of sharp and of moderate social conflict.[15]

In New Haven, in 1958, one of the first political objects to come to children's attention was the mayor; but in suburban Chicago there was little awareness of city officials during this period.[16] Recent community research has begun to specify the range of local political systems and therefore should help to provide a framework for the comparative study of political socialization.[17]

The desirability of cross-cultural research

If comparative research within a culture is likely to be instructive, comparisons between cultures seem even more promising. Although systematic cross-cultural research has only recently become common, it already has proved enormously interesting. What we take for granted within a single culture often assumes new meaning from the perspective of other cultures. A case in point is the transmission of parental party preferences to children. Many observers have commented on the "inheritance" of party loyalty in the United States, and it has been repeatedly shown that approximately three out of every four American adults have an attachment to one or the other of the major parties. But the full significance of this was not evident until comparable data became available on party identification in France. Fewer than half of the French electorate possess party identifications. Less than a third of French adults are aware of the party preferences of their parents. Thus, even when French parents *do* hold party preferences, they often fail to transmit them to their children.

Since certain of the mercurial qualities of French politics may be attributed to the weakness of party attachments in the elector-

15. Cf. Martin Levin, "Social Climates and Political Socialization," *Public Opinion Quarterly,* 25 (1961), 596–606.

16. Robert D. Hess and David Easton, "The Child's Image of the President," *Public Opinion Quarterly,* 24 (1960), 632–44.

17. Nelson Polsby, *Community Power and Political Theory* (New Haven, Yale University Press, 1963).

ate, the failure of the French family to transmit partisanship merits further study. An interesting possibility is that certain quite non-political aspects of French socialization may be at the root of this failure. Observers have pointed to the French tendency to compartmentalize the role of the child and distinguish the child's status quite sharply from that of the adult. Indirectly and inadvertently, therefore, an aspect of nonpolitical socialization may have an important effect on the functioning of French political institutions.[18]

The growth of systematic, methodologically rigorous cross-cultural research has an obvious bearing on the much maligned "national character" literature, which blossomed during and shortly after World War II. The study of national character has become somewhat unfashionable in the wake of widespread criticism of the extravagances of this literature—for example, carelessness about evidence and naïve extrapolations from infant training practices to cultural characteristics. Cross-cultural research promises to turn scholars back to the consideration of national character, but on a more empirically sound basis. Just as in the older literature, the logic of inquiry is likely to focus attention on differing socialization practices, as we attempt to explain the variations in beliefs and behavior between cultures.[19]

The need to study a wide range of political responses

The New Haven data bear on only a portion of the political orientations which can profitably be studied—mainly certain aspects of the child's feelings toward authority, information about governmental institutions and partisan politics, partisanship, and choices of exemplars. To a considerable extent we have concen-

18. See Chapter 4, pp. 77–78, esp. note 25. It should be unnecessary to say that any attempt to explain political instability in France totally (or even mainly) in terms of socialization practices would be foolish.

19. Alex Inkeles and Daniel J. Levinson, "National Character: The Study of Modal Personality and Sociocultural Systems," in *Handbook of Social Psychology, 2,* 977–1010; Bert Kaplan, *Studying Personality Cross-Culturally* (Evanston, Row, Peterson, 1961).

trated on examining the childhood precursors of active citizenship
—of participation and partisanship. Easton and Hess perform a
valuable service when they stress that the psychological aspects
of citizenship extend far beyond partisan orientations. Citizens'
attitudes and beliefs about the governmental system, the political
rules of the game, and the nation itself seem to be central to social
and political cohesion.[20] Yet they have been little studied, both
in their adult and pre-adult forms, although there has been a
scattering of thought-provoking research on the development of
national loyalty in children.[21]

The need to develop a wide range of instruments and measures

In studies of children, it is extremely important to use varied
procedures in order to avoid perseveration, responses which are
suggested by the instrument, and other sources of bias. Research
ingenuity also is essential when we study orientations which are
largely *tacit;* for example, attitudes toward authority and national
loyalty. Therefore it should be especially useful to experiment
with projective and semi-projective measures, as well as a wide
variety of explicit procedures for eliciting attitudes and beliefs.[22]
Gladys and Harold Anderson, for example, have used paragraph
completion exercises in a number of cultures to elicit orientations
toward (nonpolitical) authority. Children are presented with descriptions of a sequence of events, such as a situation in which a
schoolteacher leaves the classroom and returns to discover some

20. David Easton and Robert D. Hess, "Youth and the Political System,"
in *Culture and Social Character,* ed. Seymour M. Lipset and Leo Lowenthal,
pp. 226–51.

21. These studies have appeared in publications which ordinarily are not
consulted by students of politics. See the report of research and the sources
listed in two articles by Gustav Jahoda on "The Development of Children's
Ideas about Country and Nationality, Part I: The Conceptual Framework,"
British Journal of Educational Psychology, 33 (1963), 47–60, and "Part II:
National Symbols and Themes," ibid., 143–53.

22. For an account of such techniques, stressing the failure of many investigators to use them adequately, see Gardner Lindzey, *Projective Techniques and
Cross-Cultural Research* (New York, Appleton-Century-Crofts, 1961).

money missing from her desk. They are asked to supply the outcome to the story. The Andersons find substantial national differences in, for instance, the expectation that the child will be suspected as the culprit and will therefore be punished.[23]

I have already indicated the importance of replicating the New Haven findings with different instruments in order to determine the effects of the research technique on findings. In general, there is a need not only for study of a wide range of political responses, but also for the development of a variety of instruments for eliciting response.

The foregoing remarks on tactics of inquiry, like my discussion of the research implications of the New Haven findings, are suggestive rather than exhaustive. Hopefully they provide a sense of the rich possibilities for political socialization research. The study of the genesis of adult political behavior is certainly not a royal road to the understanding of politics. There are many obstacles to the study of children and even more to establishing in a satisfactory way the connections between early experience and later behavior. And adult behavior is affected by far more than childhood events. But if, with John Dollard, we believe that "the life of the individual is a single connected whole," it will be necessary, in order to enrich our understanding of adult political existence, "to peer down the long avenue of the individual life to see how the present-day event matured."[24]

23. See Harold H. Anderson et al., "Image of the Teacher by Adolescent Children in Four Countries: Germany, England, Mexico, United States," *Journal of Social Psychology, 50* (1959), 47–55. The Andersons have kindly made available to me certain unpublished portions of their data. Also Kenneth W. Terhune, "An Examination of Some Contributing Demographic Variables in a Cross-National Study," *Journal of Social Psychology, 59* (1963), 209–19. For an interesting projective technique for eliciting children's feelings about their own importance in relation to authority figures see John L. Kennedy and Harold D. Lasswell, "A Cross-Cultural Test of Self-Image," *Human Organization, 17* (1958), 41–43.

24. John Dollard, *Criteria for the Life History* (New Haven, Yale University Press, 1935), p. 27.

Postscript on the Educational Implications of
Political Socialization Research

*When this work was originally in preparation, one editorial
suggestion to which I found myself unwilling to respond was that
I discuss the practical implications of my findings for educational
policy. It was not that I thought the assignment a poor one but that
I felt uncomfortable about carrying it out. The following reflections on that sense of difficulty, which bear generally on the connection between social research and social policy, were stimulated
by the experience (shortly after the publication of* Children and
Politics, *in 1965) of serving as a consultant to an incipient civic
education program. I prepared these remarks in late 1965, and
their tone reflects the sense of disengagement that many social
scientists then felt. Through the vagaries of academic publishing,
they appeared in print four years later, at which time much had
transpired: on university campuses, in South East Asia, and in
America's black ghettoes. Indeed the heat of events had nearly
driven from the lexicon one of the central terms in what follows:
the word "Negro." Yet in spite of the social engagement of much of
the discourse of 1969, I do not feel that my message—which is that
we need* reasoned *applications of social knowledge to social policy
—is obsolete. This postscript also, incidentally, notes some of the
main contributions to political socialization research since the
original report of my New Haven study. It is slightly modified from
the form it took in* The School Review, *77 (1969), 41–53, where
it was entitled "The Case of the Reluctant Consultant: On Moving
from What We Know to What We Ought to Do" (copyright
1969 by the University of Chicago). I am indebted to the publisher
of that journal, the University of Chicago Press, for permission to
reprint the article here.*

Not long ago I had an experience which brought home the relevance for social science of Thurber's art expert who "knows all about art, but doesn't know what he likes." I was asked to suggest a program of action to foster public political participation. The request was made by a committee of academics from another university. The members of this committee felt that their university would better discharge its obligations if it were to enter the field which is variously called political education, civic education, and education for citizenship.

Since the quality of public political participation in the United States is scarcely inspiring, it would have been difficult not to sympathize with the committee's desire to take action. About four out of every ten Americans failed to vote in the last presidential election. Typically, somewhat less than half of the adult electorate bothers to go to the polls in the off-year congressional elections. Activities more demanding than voting are even less frequently performed; for example, writing to public officials, ringing doorbells for a political party, contributing money to political causes are all pursuits of a small minority (5–15 per cent) of the public. And just as the extent of public political participation falls far enough short of democratic ideals to provide educators with an ample agenda, so does the extent of political enlightenment. Public opinion polls show that most citizens have a scanty supply of information about public affairs and that many of the very principles which would seem to be at the heart of democratic politics (e.g., willingness to let unpopular minorities express themselves) are not widely shared.[1]

Over the years there have been numerous efforts to rectify this state of affairs: public information programs, voter registration campaigns, well-financed non-partisan efforts to persuade every-

1. For the sources of my various observations about adult political participation, see, for example, Robert E. Lane, *Political Life* (New York, Free Press, 1959); Angus Campbell et al., *The American Voter* (New York, John Wiley & Sons, 1960); Fred I. Greenstein, *The American Party System and the American People* (Englewood Cliffs, N.J., Prentice-Hall, 1963, 2d ed. 1970), Chapters 2 and 3.

body to vote for "the party of your choice," programs focusing on special groups of "potential leaders," such as businessmen or college students, movements to revise the grade school and high school social studies curriculum. Yet wherever it has been possible to observe the effects of these programs, the evidence has been that their impact is slim or nonexistent. For example, in spite of the considerable activity of groups such as the American Heritage Society, the level of voting—and of abstention from voting—has been quite stable over the past decade.

By and large, these programs have a common deficiency. They do not proceed within a frame of reference which takes detailed account of the dynamics of the political behavior they attempt to change. The programs have little or no basis in the social psychology of political participation and political apathy. Failing to begin from an understanding of such matters as who participates in politics, who fails to participate, and why, the educator is unable to pinpoint his targets and gear his efforts to their special requirements.

All of this would have been quite understandable several decades ago, when little was known about the dynamics of public political participation. Today, as a result of a spate of research into public opinion, electoral behavior, and other participation patterns, much is known. Studies have been made which provide us with detailed evidence of who in the electorate is politically active in what ways: the psychologies of various groupings of citizens (for example, the highly apathetic, apolitical segment of the electorate) have been examined with some care; information has accumulated about the effects of efforts by mass communication and other means to increase information and to change attitudes and behavior; the determinants of public opinion and electoral behavior now have been studied extensively in the United States and to a lesser degree elsewhere in the world. Furthermore, a recent eddy of research, going under the label "political socialization," with which I have been connected for the past several years, has sought to establish how citizenship develops in the life cycle and what patterns of experience from childhood on are conducive to various levels of adult political participation.[2]

PROFESSIONAL UNEASINESS

Knowing of these developments, the committee felt that the time was ripe for new departures in an activity which has not been conspicuous for its sophistication or its success—civic education. And it seemed a not unreasonable assumption that people who had been active in contributing to this research would be able to suggest promising directions for action. Eventually I *did* suggest a program, but only after subjecting the committee to certain laborious intellectual convolutions. The shift from being an ostensibly neutral student of political dynamics to recommending policy based on research of mine and of others was, I found, the source of considerable professional uneasiness. Furthermore, it was precisely the intellectual habits that had provided me with some appreciation of how political change might be effected which led to my uneasiness about moving from contemplation to action.

If this experience of being a reluctant consultant was only autobiographical, it would be of no great interest. It is not, and therein lies the point. A recent book by David Braybrooke and Charles E. Lindblom begins with the following passage:

> A curious paradox bedevils social scientists and others involved in the evaluation and choice of policies. They habitually resort to certain practices that enable them to cope with the task of organizing information in ways relevant to making policy decision. Yet their conceptions of evaluation and de-

2. On political socialization, in addition to the study of New Haven children in the present volume, see Robert D. Hess and Judith V. Torney, *The Development of Political Attitudes in Children* (Chicago, Aldine Publishing Co., 1967); David Easton and Jack Dennis, *Children and the Political System* (New York, McGraw-Hill, 1969); and the various sources cited in Jack Dennis' valuable *A Survey and Bibliography of Contemporary Research on Political Learning and Socialization* (Madison, Wisconsin Research and Development Center for Cognitive Learning, Occasional Paper No. 8, 1967).

cision-making typically imply contempt for these practices.
For the most part, this discrepancy goes unnoticed and un-
explained. It is reflected, however, in the uneasiness which
people, especially social scientists, often display while they
are engaged in evaluation. . . .

Consider the troubled mien with which the economist
often leaves a congressional committee-room, however ably
he has testified there. He may have spoken as pertinently and
pointedly on behalf of a certain proposal for closing loop-
holes in the income tax laws as anyone could. Yet he won-
ders, on leaving, whether he has not, under the pressure of
time and circumstance, sacrificed professional ideals. Has he
not perhaps swept beyond the bounds of his professional
competence to give expert advice? Has he not mixed the empirical and evaluative aspects of the question too freely? Has
he failed to give the committee due notice that his criteria for
policy are criteria that the committee might repudiate? Has
he failed to clarify the hypotheses and qualifications required
to make his testimony sound?

The same uneasiness, which we take to be a symptom of
the discrepancy between practice and ideal, may be illustrated
in the sophisticated second thoughts by the author and the
scientific public about (say) a journal article proposing a
special curriculum for bright students in the public schools.
The argument in the article may be cogent and perceptive.
Its author may, by all ordinary, nonprofessional standards of
analysis, appear to have gone to the heart of the matter. Yet,
what if the article is tested against the standards of thorough-
ness that social science and philosophy have established for
the evaluation of decision-making? The author has not exhausted all of the considerations relevant to choosing a new
curriculum in preference to others that might be designed
to serve the same ends. He has not, for that matter, fully described what his ends are or worked out a scheme for coordi-
nating them in all the circumstances that may arise. If this
argument is convincing, it is convincing without his having

gone through the standard operations generally prescribed for rational decision-making.[3]

I can illustrate these assertions of Braybrooke and Lindblom by recapitulating the rather labored memorandum I presented to the committee. What we see is: (1) a somewhat agonized attempt to attack the problem in what Braybrooke and Lindblom call a "synoptic" fashion—that is, taking account of the full complexity of the problem, with exhausting if not exhaustive attention to qualifications; (2) a selective résumé of relevant research; (3) a proposal for action, "arbitrarily" wrested from the vast universe of possible actions; (4) a final (and, I think, at least partially constructive) obeisance to the ideal of comprehensiveness and intellectual fastidiousness.

A Synoptic View of Civic Education

I began the memorandum with two definitions of civic education and an observation based on the gap between them. The first defines civic education narrowly, as we normally conceive of it in curriculum guides on the topic and in, for example, the statutory provisions made by virtually every state for "education for citizenship": "the deliberate inculcation of civic information, values, and practices by instructional agents who have been formally charged with this responsibility."

The second, broader conception is one that has emerged from the recent research on political socialization. This research has been concerned not only with the effects of the schools on individuals, but also with the entire complex of antecedents of adult political behavior: *"all* determinants of civic learning: unplanned, as well as deliberate; informal as well as formal; learning at every stage of the life cycle, including learning which is nominally unconnected with civic behavior, but which affects civic behavior (for example, the acquisition of relevant personality dispositions)."

3. David Braybrooke and Charles E. Lindblom, *Strategy of Decision* (New York, Free Press, 1963), pp. 3–4.

The first of these definitions, I pointed out, rules out of consideration the great bulk of learning which, as far as we can tell from present research, actually molds the individual's adult political actions. What kind of adult political participant (or nonparticipant) we become is largely dependent on such factors as our socioeconomic background, family and neighborhood experiences, and contact with the mass media. The educational *level* we attain is highly relevant to our adult political behavior—education provides skills and opportunities which are conducive to political participation. But there is little evidence that the educational programs explicitly directed toward citizenship, as presently constituted, have much of an impact upon political participation. As Mr. Dooley replied, when asked if education is responsible for "the progress of the world," "D'ye think 'tis th' mill that makes th' wather run?"

If, then, the committee was thinking of instituting classroom civic education programs, one of the contributions of the expert on these matters would be this dampener: "Present evidence is that such programs are not likely to have significant impact."[4] (The fact that *current* programs are ineffective is, of course, no argument against improving future programs. But the fact that so much of the basis for civic behavior is independent of the schools *does* lead us to suspect that efforts to influence political participation cannot depend exclusively upon formal educational programs.)

But this only begins the qualifications. A section of the memorandum entitled "A Comprehensive Context for Thinking about Civic Education" began with two remarks on "the place of civic education in the social process." The first was that political behavior depends on more than those elements "within the skin" of the individual, which result from his educational experiences—even conceiving these broadly in terms of the totality of his political socialization. Behavior depends not only on the individual's

4. Kenneth P. Langton and M. Kent Jennings, "Political Socialization and the High School Civics Curriculum in the United States," *American Political Science Review,* 62 (September 1964), 852–67.

predispositions, but also on the situations within which he finds himself. Therefore, the memorandum continued, "for some purposes (such as increasing political participation) it may be more economical to restructure situations (e.g., to simplify voter registration procedures) than to bring about changes in individual predispositions through education." It is, of course, precisely this kind of situational change which the federal government has from time to time attempted to effect in the South with respect to Negro voting. But, in addition to the situational influences, much of the change in Negro political participation (including the willingness of the federal government to act) is a result of the striking predispositional changes which are summed up in the shorthand expression "the Negro revolution."

My second remark under this heading was to point out that "there is no one-to-one connection between individual behavior and the functioning of social (including political) institutions." One of the programs the committee had thought of sponsoring involved increasing public appreciation of the notion of due process of law. In a further access of scholarly pessimism, I wanted to point out that a simple shift in public attitudes toward some institution, such as the courts, would not automatically have an impact on how that institution functioned. Institutions are sheltered, often advisedly, from the direct and immediate impact of public opinion.

Then I turned to a formulation of "the context for planning civic education programs," which was synoptic with a vengeance. Harold D. Lasswell is by all counts one of the more comprehensive thinkers in the social sciences. He also is distinguished for his repeated emphasis on the desirability of organizing and conducting social science as a "policy science"—that is, of carrying out social inquiry and social policy in intimate connection with each other. Five basic intellectual operations, Lasswell argues, are entailed in what he calls a "configurative" approach to uniting theory and practice: (1) developing general scientific knowledge—that is, empirical theory—bearing on the problem at hand; (2) ascertaining past and present historical trends; (3) using the general knowledge about underlying processes (a) to extrapolate from the past trends (*b*) in order to make predictions about the likely future state of affairs, in the absence of any attempt to redirect the trend; (4) positing goals—that is, the statement of normative theory; and (5) finally, of course, the actual invention of policy alternative designed to redirect the trends toward the goals.[5]

Using this classification as my basis, I suggested that the committee's interest in the fifth class of activity—designing programs —could ideally be seen as fitting into the following matrix of intellectual operations.

A codification of our present general propositions bearing upon civic development.—For this it would be necessary to draw upon quite disparate research in such fields as education, communication and persuasion, child development, public opinion and voting, political socialization, and political recruitment.

An inventory of past and present historical trends in civic education, as broadly conceived.—This could be organized on some basis such as the following: "Who has been educated, in what way, by what agents, with what effects on the individual's later behavior and on society."

Alternative models of likely future trends.—Here there should also be some estimate of the probabilities.

Sophisticated clarification of the goals of civic education.—This would involve not simply a ceremonial abstract listing of "that which we hold dear," but rather a detailed consideration of short-run and long-run objectives, with particular attention given to conflicts among goals, all of which may in principle be desirable, but some of which are to varying degrees incompatible with others. There may, for example, be a conflict between the ideal of a politically active electorate and that of a politically informed electorate: increasing voter turnout may involve decreasing the average level of voter information.

Of course, all of the foregoing should be done with meticulous standards of rigor and, where relevant, evidence.

5. See, for example, Harold D. Lasswell, "Strategies of Inquiry: The Rational Use of Observation," in Daniel Lerner, ed., *The Human Meaning of the Social Sciences* (New York, Meridian Books, 1959), pp. 89–113.

As I have already said, an impressive amount of information relevant to any program of education for political activity now has accumulated. In fact, there have been striking recent advances bearing on this formulation of "the context" which I have not referred to, especially a recent burgeoning of writings on democratic theory. Yet what strikes one about the list is *not* how much we can say in each of its categories, but rather how little. Most of our general propositions are not very general and are at best hypotheses, in the most tentative sense of the word. By and large the hypotheses and our descriptive trend data are based on limited studies of limited populations. My own work on political socialization is, to take an obvious instance, based on a single study of elementary school children conducted a number of years ago in a single community. The construction of carefully reasoned estimates of future trends is an intermittent activity of a few scholars and others with visionary tendencies. And much of the existing normative discussion, though soulful, does not go far beyond the level of platitude.

To make matters worse, it is not clear how some of the tasks implicit in such an agenda would be carried out and with what success. How do we draw boundaries around our codification of propositions, or our inventory of trends? An even more vexed issue is that of stating normative goals. Some social scientists, taking their cue from certain early statements of logical positivism, would hold that there is nothing whatsoever they can contribute in their professional capacities to this activity. (The well-known dependence of businessmen on dead economists may well have its parallel in the tendency of social scientists to ground their beliefs on the work of outmoded philosophers.) Even scholars who hold that value and fact are irreconcilably separate would, however, be reluctant simply to accept received value premises and devise policies to advance them.

Most social scientists would of course (in practice if not in proclamation) acknowledge the sterility of discussions of normative goals which are totally independent of empirical relevance. Goals, if they are to be more than an exercise in piety, need to be

considered in terms of what presently exists, the likely consequences of the present state of affairs, and the likely consequences
of alternative states of affairs. And, as I have suggested, the really
tough normative questions are not about single goals in splendid
isolation, but about the conflicts, at the margins, between goals:
How much freedom are we willing to give up for some further
degree of security, or vice versa? How much are we willing to give
up if we already have high levels of security (or freedom)? Or if
the level of one or the other is low?

Many of these questions, Lindblom and Braybrooke argue, are
in their general form not answerable *in principle,* much less in
practice—independent of some concrete policy problem. The set
of "alternative states of affairs" is logically unbounded and presumably infinite, since policy proposals can be permuted and combined in endless ways. Outside of the limited sphere of economics,
it is not clear how to assign utility functions to values. (For a fuller
statement on the shortcomings in principle of a synoptic approach,
see Braybrooke and Lindblom.) But whether or not there are logical limits to a full configurative treatment, there are limits in practice. All of the steps involve costly allocations of effort, and effort,
scholarly and otherwise, is in limited supply. Even with enormous
social resources devoted to the problem of civic education (and
after all, there *are* other problems), if the relevant context had to
be "fully" filled in before taking action, either no action would
occur or, by the time we were ready to institute a program, the
situation would have changed.[6]

PRESCRIPTION FOR POLICY: SIMPLY BEGIN!

At this point my memorandum underwent a sharp and rather
ungainly transition. Having outlined, at a high level of abstrac-
tion, what seemed to me to be the major broad analytic considera-
ations governing the interplay of research and policy in the area

6. I should note that Lasswell himself does not argue that policy decisions
must be delayed until the remainder of the configuration is filled in. Rather,
he favors systematic experimental introduction of policies and their assessment—a position quite in harmony with that of Braybrooke and Lindblom.

of civic education, I found that I had acquired an interesting increment of self-awareness. Doing this made explicit for me something of which I had so far been only imperfectly aware—namely, why in my previous writing on political socialization I had been unwilling to discuss policy implications of my findings. The standards of comprehensiveness I had come to accept as necessary for intelligent discourse were paralyzing when it came to proposing action. I then turned to Braybrooke and Lindblom's reminder that social scientists and others, after all, *do* "habitually resort to certain practices that enable them to cope with the task of organizing information in ways relevant to making policy decisions," in the process necessarily abandoning their standards of "total" comprehensiveness. This is an obvious statement, but one which has the same freshness of vision as the small boy's observation of the unclothed emperor.

I will not attempt to recapitulate all of Braybrooke and Lindblom's statements about the "habitual practices" which actually are used to recommend and make policy. These include introducing some policy intervention at the point where a readily recognizable problem, or "evil," can be seen; attacking problems which are within our resources, and willingness, to attack; making frequent use of social techniques with which we have some experience; and instituting programs bit by bit, observing the consequences, including those which were unanticipated, and then making corrections. All of this is not unlike the definition of democracy attributed to William James: a system in which the government does something and sees who hollers. Hence my transitional statement:

> Yet it would be foolish to suggest that no useful civic education programs can be launched without first engaging in the kind of exhaustive analysis implied by [my initial statement of the context]. A typical—and not undesirable—way of beginning a program is *simply to begin:* i.e., to choose some target of opportunity (a situation which is manifestly problematic, which can command the enthusiastic participation of the program's staff, and which is within their resources).

PROPOSITIONS AND A PROPOSAL

Most of the remainder of the memorandum consisted of propositions extracted selectively from the relevant social science literature, with particular emphasis on findings which seemed to me to
have been ignored by previous citizenship programs and, more
especially, on findings bearing on my own proposal, which was
directed at reaching groups that are especially poorly integrated
into the American political system. First we may consider some of
the propositions.

1. There are very striking differences in political involvement,
information, and participation from group to group in the United
States. To take only one handy indication, we might consider
participation in presidential elections. In 1960, the following three
partially overlapping categories of citizens stood at the top of a
ranking of groups by their turnout in the presidential election:
College educated (90 per cent voted); professional and managerial
occupations (88 per cent); other white-collar workers (84 per
cent). At the other end of the ranking were three different, and
also overlapping, groupings: Unskilled workers (68 per cent
voted); grade school educated (67 per cent); Negroes (54 per
cent).

2. Many of the existing programs designed to foster political
participation have concentrated on making broad, "across the
board" appeals to all population groups, appealing to the citizen's
"duty" to be politically active, rather than isolating specific target
groups. Other programs, proceeding on the assumption that certain classes of individuals are the society's "natural leaders," have
focused on precisely those categories which are already most active
relative to others in the society—for example, the college educated
and business executives. Programs focusing on the groups which
actually are low in participation have until recently been rare, the
main exception being the effort of organized labor to get out the
vote of its membership. Recently, of course, we have seen systematic effort to increase Negro political participation, especially
in the South, and the controversial and evidently rather chaotic

efforts to mobilize politically the citizens affected by federal poverty programs.

3. Wherever it has been possible to assess the effectiveness of the programs designed to increase citizens' political involvement and their general willingness to participate (as opposed simply to one-shot programs to get voters to the polls, or attempts to remove mechanical restrictions on participation), the results have proved to be minimal or nonexistent. Several reasons for this can be suggested:

a) "Across the board" programs of exhortation are subject to all of the factors which make propaganda by mass communication an inefficient technique for changing beliefs and behavior. To begin with, the message tends largely to be received by those who are already sympathetic to it and therefore least in need of change. For the remainder of the population, the message is ignored, "crowded out" by other more potent communications, or even misperceived. When it is taken in, it is not reinforced at the face-to-face level and nothing is done to change the individual's actual life situation in order to facilitate acting on the message.[7]

b) Many of the same difficulties attend the occasional programs which have been directed toward low-participation groups: there is too much attention to general exhortation and too little effort made to tailor the program in some precise way to those aspects of the individual and his situation which impede participation.

c) Programs designed to increase the participation of groups which are already relatively active may run aground not only for the foregoing reasons but also because the potentialities for participation have already been largely exhausted in these groups. If, for example, 90 per cent of the college educated already vote, it is likely that the remaining 10 per cent will not readily yield to an educational program. This residual group probably includes individuals who for various technical reasons are unable to partici-

7. Herbert H. Hyman and Paul B. Sheatsley, "Some Reasons Why Information Campaigns Fail," *Public Opinion Quarterly, 11* (Fall 1947), 412–23; Joseph T. Klapper, *The Effects of Mass Communication* (New York, Free Press, 1960).

pate, people with personality characteristics leading to extreme withdrawal from social life, individuals who are ideologically alienated from the political system, and so forth.

d) A further probable reason for the ineffectiveness of political education programs is suggested by the recent research on children's political orientations. Such programs seem to come too late in life. Much of the learning relevant to adult civic behavior takes place quite early in childhood—before the age at which the child is normally exposed to formal civic training. For example, attachments to political parties are formed largely on a basis quite like the "inheritance" of family religious affiliations, by the early grade school years. During these years children, although their information about politics is at best rudimentary, often respond with enthusiastic partisanship to the stimulus of election campaigns.

e) When children are finally exposed to explicit civic education (typically between the sixth and eighth grades), the exposure is largely to information about the formal machinery of government. Little effort is made to capture whatever spontaneous impulses the child does have toward political involvement. In civic education programs designed for children (and, as well, in the bulk of programs directed at adults) the emphasis is on emotionally neutral, non-partisan appeals to participate out of a sense of obligation. Yet, on the evidence of the research which has been done on voter motivations, partisan enthusiasm seems to be one of the stronger determinants of political participation.

4. As would be expected from the observation that political involvement develops relatively early in childhood, group differences in political involvement also have early roots. Thus the differences in the participation rates between upper and lower socioeconomic status group adults, which we have already noted, are paralleled by a variety of differences in the political orientations of high and low social status children. Similarly, women are less politically active than men, and sex differences in political interest and information can be found among children as young as nine years of age.

5. Childhood group differences in political involvement (to re-

turn to a point made earlier about the importance of informal extra-school political socialization) have substantial non-political as well as political sources. That is, although part of the reason for the lower political involvement of lower-class children is simply that their parents and other environmental influences expose them to less information, there are other less directly political reasons: They do not acquire the skills in manipulation of symbols which foster attention to politics. And there are even more profound psychological consequences of the class differences in child raising. Lower-status children are reared in ways which provide them with less independence of thought and greater willingness to defer to authority than higher-status children. As Robert E. Lane puts it, "Child-rearing practices in the lower-status groups tend to provide a less adequate personality basis for appropriately self-assertive social participation. . . . In general, the middle-class child seems to receive, at the same time, greater encouragement to explore and be ambitious, and greater capacity for internal regulation and purposive action."[8] The impact of non-political factors is even more striking in the case of sex differences in children's political involvement, since boys and girls are exposed to roughly the same political information. What seems to be crucial here is the early learning of sex roles which orient boys to aspects of the wider environment—including politics—and which direct the interest and attention of girls more to matters domestic.

Then, on the basis of this admittedly rather selective foray into the recent social science literature, I proceeded to sketch very roughly what my conception would be of an interesting and fruitful program:

> It might well be decided that the likely targets of opportunity are groups such as the three referred to above, ranking lowest in political participation: unskilled workers, grade-school educated, and Negroes. Work with such groups and their children would bring out rather starkly the problem raised earlier in this memorandum about the relative import-

8. Lane, p. 234.

ance of formal educational and other influences on civic behavior. The chances are slim that narrowly conceived classroom programs for encouraging civic participation would be
especially successful in influencing such groups. One would
have to think in more comprehensive terms, reaching beyond
civic education of the traditional sort: It might, for example,
be necessary to formulate programs which raised such individuals' general aspirational levels and educational attain-
ments, such as the New York Higher Horizons programs
and the various recent poverty program experiments; programs which enlisted both parents and their children; programs which went beyond the classroom in facilitating participation and reinforcing the desire to participate.

There would be little sense, at the committee's stage in its de-
liberations, in my going beyond this sketchy suggestion of a target
and the broad tack which might be taken in attempting to work
with it. Clearly the committee was not compelled, logically or
otherwise, to take an interest in my proposal. It might have other
ideas. It might reject certain of the goals implicit in my proposal.
For example, one short-run consequence of such a program, if
successful, would be to increase the vote for Democrats, at least
in national elections. Another, which I have alluded to, would be
to expand the segment of the voting public which tends to be low
in political information. My view is that these considerations
would be overweighed by positive outcomes: a broadening of the
base of the political system; an increasing tendency for politicians
to attend to the wants of groups which hitherto could have been
more safely ignored; at any rate, by this point in the memorandum
I had worked my way around to the point of mastering my professional phobia about offering policy advice. Furthermore, I had
worked my way around to a general proposal which I—and, I
hoped, the committee—found ethically congenial, challenging,
and intellectually interesting, and which was, since it was so much
within the ambit of the current national social preoccupations, a
program which seemed practically feasible.

OBEISANCE TO THE SYNOPTIC IDEAL

As I have suggested, the arguments of Braybrooke and Lindblom were therapeutic for me. In this instance of a discrepancy between the scholarly ideal and actual practice, their argument ran, it was the ideal which was at fault. I think they are right, but in part they may be insufficiently sensitive to certain merits of the ideal—not its "official" merits, but certain of its incidental consequences. Comprehensive formulations such as the one I began with provide, I think, not standards to be attained, but rather useful background exercises—intellectual prophylactics. Master plans and other utopias are mind-stretching devices—ways of getting perspective and suggesting connections and contingencies. In current jargon, they are heuristic. Among other things, by setting up synoptic goals, they remind us to stretch ourselves and to try in our less-than-utopian way to get the most out of our efforts. And, even though such goals are unattainable in detail, the partially spurious sense of "vision" they provide serves to energize us for the day-to-day efforts that go into making incremental advances. Therefore, just after deprecating my contextual formulation and proposing "simply to begin," I added a further statement deferring to the ideal:

What *would* be desirable is to design any program so that it proceeds in a sophisticated, intellectually productive manner, enabling it—apart from its specific effects on whatever groups actually are worked with—to fill in the broader context for thought and action in the area of civic education. Efforts to bring about change can be closely allied to efforts to fill in the intellectual map in an ever more comprehensive fashion. They also need not depart from scholarly demands for clarity and for careful attention to evidence and inference. For example, by treating any project as a vehicle for careful research, it becomes in effect a demonstration project, and therefore can have an effect well beyond its immediate impact on the participants. Rigorous assessment of the project's strong and weak points (if possible by incorporating some of the features of classical experimental design) is therefore highly desirable. Too many "do-good" activities are vitiated by lack of firm information about their effects. And too many programs limp along with the *desirability* of their effects and the alternative directions they might take, never receiving a reflective assessment.

Appendix A

Civic Responsibility Interview

Answer Sheet Part I

Name .... Address ....
      (First name)   (Last name)

Age ...., Ages of brothers (if any) ...., Ages of sisters (if any) ....

Boy .... Girl .... Teacher ....

In what country did *most* of your relatives live before they came to America? (check one)

England .... Ireland .... Italy .... Poland ....

Some other country ....
                      (Write in name of country—do not put in United States)

Don't know ....

---

1. What do you like to do most when there is no school? (Write in one thing) ....
....

2. If you could have *one* wish and it would come true, what would you wish? ....
....

3. How many friends do you like to be with after school? (Check one)

    very large group ....

    large group ....

    few friends ....

    yourself ....

*The questionnaire is in two parts. Parts one and two were administered on successive weeks in Schools A, B, and C. Both parts were administered the same day in School D.

4. Whom do you like to be with most on weekends? (Check one)

   your friends ....

   your family ....

   yourself ....

5. Do you like to talk much with your friends? (Check one)

   yes .... no ....

6. Who are your two best friends *in this class?*

   (1) ....

   (2) ....

7. Do you think children are punished too much?

   yes .... no .... don't know ....

8. When do you watch TV?

   (1) Do you watch in the morning (before school)?

   never .... sometimes .... every day .... (check one)

   (2) Do you watch in the afternoon (after school)?

   never .... sometimes .... every day .... (check one)

   (3) Do you watch in the evening (after eating?)

   never .... sometimes .... every day .... (check one)

9. Which do you like most?

   (1) reading books .... or going to the movies ....? (check one)

   (2) sports .... or reading books ....? (check one)

   (3) reading books .... or helping with work at home ....?

   (check one)

10. How many comic books did you read last week? (circle the number)

    0 1 2 3 4 5 6 7 8 9 10 11 12 13 14 15 16 17 18 19 20 ....

11. When was the last time that you read a news story on the front page of the newspaper?

    yesterday or today .... in the last week .... before the last week .... never ....

12. Can you think of a news story which interested you? Tell what it was about. (This can be from the newspaper or from the news on radio or TV.) ....

    ....

    ....

13. Can you think of a news story which made you feel happy?

    ....

    ....

14. Can you think of a news story which made you feel angry?

....

....

15. Name a famous person you want to be like:

    (1) ....

    Name a famous person you *don't* want to be like:

    (2) ....

16. Which place would you rather read a news story about? (check one)

    New Haven ....

    Washington, D.C. ....

17. Which school subjects do you like most?

    (1) arithmetic .... or social studies ....? (check one)

    (2) social studies .... or spelling ....? (check one)

    (3) art .... or social studies ....? (check one)

18. Do you have any lessons out of school? (music lessons, religious training, etc.) Write in the kinds of lessons you have and what day you have them.

    Kind of lessons   Day you have them

    (1) ....

    (2) ....

    (3) ....

    (4) ....

19. What you think of people:

    (1) Check the names of the *four* most important people:

    Mayor of a city ....

    Schoolteacher ....

    Judge ....

    School principal ....

    President of the country ....

    Doctor ....

    Police chief ....

    Religious leader ....

    (2) Check *four* names many people are afraid of:

    Mayor of a city ....

    Schoolteacher ....

    Judge ....

    School principal ....

    President of the country ....

Doctor ....
Police chief ....
Religious leader ....

(3) Check all the jobs you would like when you are older. (Girls can also check jobs they would want their husbands to have.)
Mayor of a city ....
Schoolteacher ....
Judge ....
School principal ....
President of the country ....
Doctor ....
Police chief ....
Religious leader ....

20. Can you think of another job you would like? ....

CIVIC RESPONSIBILITY INTERVIEW

Answer Sheet Part II

Name .... Teacher ....
     (First name)   (Last name)

Example one

Who is the Superintendent of Schools?
a. His name is ....
b. Never heard of the Superintendent of Schools ....
c. Can't think of his name ....

Example two

What kinds of things do you think the Chief of Police does? ....
....

Example three

What kind of an athlete do you think Mickey Mantle is?
don't know .... very good .... fairly good .... not very good .... bad ....

1. Who is the Mayor of New Haven?
   a. His name is ....
   b. Never heard of the Mayor ....
   c. Can't think of his name ....
2. What kinds of things do you think the Mayor does? ....
....

3. What kind of a job has the Mayor been doing?
   don't know ...... very good ...... fairly good ...... not very good ......
   bad ......

4. Here are the names of some people from your section of New Haven who have been in the news lately. Have you heard of any of these people? If you have, circle the name of *one* person you know and tell why he has been in the news.

The people	*Why in the news?*
[Names of local aldermen	....
were typed in here]	....

4a. Have you heard of the New Haven Board of Aldermen?
    yes .... no ....
    What does the Board of Aldermen do? ....

5. Who is the Governor of Connecticut?
   a. His name is ....
   b. Never heard of the Governor ....
   c. Can't think of his name ....

6. What kinds of things does the Governor do? ....

7. What kind of job has the Governor been doing?
   don't know ...... very good ...... fairly good ...... not very good ......
   bad ......

8. Have you heard of the Connecticut General Assembly? (Also called the State Legislature)
   yes .... no ....
   What does it do? ....

9. Who is the President of the United States?
   a. His name is ....
   b. Never heard of the President ....
   c. Can't think of his name ....

10. What kinds of things do you think the President does? ....

11. What kind of a job has the President been doing?
    don't know ...... very good ...... fairly good ...... not very good ......
    bad ......

11a. Adlai Stevenson ran for president in 1956. *If* he had been elected, what kind of a job do you think he would have done?

don't know ...... very good ...... fairly good ...... not very good ......
bad ......

12. Have you heard of Congress? (Also called the Senate and the House of Representatives)
yes .... no ....
What does Congress do? ....
....

13. Questions about elections:
    (1) Not everyone who is 21 votes at election time. Will you vote when you are 21?
    yes .... no .... don't know ....
    (2) Tell who won the election you remember best: ....
....
    (3) Do you think it makes much difference which side wins an election?
    yes .... no ....

14. The Democrats and Republicans:
Who do you think is the most famous Democrat? ....
Who do you think is the most famous Republican? ....

14a. Can you think of a difference between the Democrats and Republicans? ....

15. If you were 21 now, whom would you vote for most of the time? (check one)
mostly Republicans ....
mostly Democrats ....
don't know ....

16. Whom do you think your friends would vote for? (check one)
mostly Republicans ....
mostly Democrats ....
don't know ....

17. Whom do you think your parents would vote for, if there were an election today?

	FATHER	MOTHER
mostly Republicans	....	....
mostly Democrats	....	....
don't know	....	....

18. If you could vote, who would be best to ask for voting advice? (check one)
a friend your own age ....

    brother or sister ....

    father ....

    mother ....

    teacher ....

    someone else ....

             (Write in whether this person is a neighbor, relative, or what.)

19. If you could change the world in any way you wanted, what change would you make?

....

....

Thank you for your help in this project.

Appendix B

Where appropriate I have referred briefly in the text to the research procedure used in this study of the political socialization of New Haven, Connecticut, elementary school children. Appendix B serves to recapitulate and enlarge upon procedural questions relating to the conception, design, and execution of the New Haven research, as well as the composition of the sample.

Design and conception. Because of the absence of research and theory on political socialization, the New Haven study was of necessity exploratory. The main purpose was to gather preliminary normative data on the development of political involvement and awareness and to distill hypotheses from these observations. With few exceptions, explicit a priori hypotheses were not formulated and tested. Rather, a broad conception of the aspects of political socialization which seemed to merit investigation served to guide the study. Questions such as the following were the basis for developing a research instrument: How much awareness of the adult political process is there during the elementary school years? Which aspects of politics are children aware of? What is the content of children's perceptions of politics? What is the nature of their affective orientations toward such aspects of politics as the parties, public officials, etc.? How does political learning vary with age and with the child's other social and psychological characteristics?

Since considerable research had been done on *adult* electoral behavior, data were available on the terminus of one aspect of political learning. Therefore it was expedient to study childhood precursors of voting motivation. In a study of children, it also is more important to concentrate on the level and content of political information than would be the case in research on adults, where it ordinarily is assumed (sometimes with insufficient warrant) that a basic awareness of the structure of government and politics is present. And a good bit of the questionnaire necessarily was composed of items which were not explicitly political in content—for example, indicators of possible determinants of political development.

Preliminary field work began in the summer of 1957 with loosely structured, exploratory interviews. Chapter 2 illustrates the technique of these interviews: I recited a series of terms relating to the major aspects of American government and politics, asking the child to comment on the meaning of the terms, and "what they make you think of," attempting as far as possible to avoid suggesting responses and probing for further clarification where appropriate. Partly to establish rapport and partly to see whether spontaneous references to politics might be elicited, the political portions of the interviews were preceded by a good bit of nonpolitical questioning (not reported in Chapter 2) about after-school activities, preferred school subjects, media behavior, etc.

A preliminary paper-and-pencil questionnaire then was drafted on the basis of the initial interviewing. This and later drafts of the questionnaire followed the funnel effect described above of beginning with the nonpolitical and continuing toward increasingly explicit political questioning. Since classroom time was not always available for administration of the entire questionnaire in one session, the form was divided into two parts. After a pretest administration of the initial questionnaire in the fourth, fifth, and sixth grade classrooms of a moderate-to-low-income New Haven school, I analyzed responses and individually interviewed a number of the respondents. A revised questionnaire form then was drafted in which ambiguous or otherwise unsatisfactory items were eliminated or altered. The revised form was administered to an additional pretest group, fifth graders in a moderate income East Haven, Connecticut, community. Pretesting took place during the fall of 1957. The pretesting, in addition to leading to modifications of the questionnaire, made it possible to perfect the mechanics of administering questionnaires to entire classrooms. (Personal interviewing was not feasible in the final study beyond a dozen follow-up interviews which served as a rough check on the reliability and stability of questionnaire responses.)

Administration procedure. The final form of the questionnaire was administered to the fourth through eighth grade children of four

New Haven schools in widely diversified socioeconomic areas between January and March of 1958. (The composition of the sample is discussed below.) When I administered the questionnaires to classrooms, my introductory remarks stressed that "this is not a test" and emphasized that "nobody at school will see your answers." After the presentation of the instructions it was possible for children in grades six through eight to self-administer the questionnaires. In the fourth and fifth grades, items were read aloud in the classroom. The children were cautioned not to answer out loud; they were instructed to raise their hands if they had questions about the meaning of items or the spelling of names and these questions were answered, *sotto voce,* by the teacher or by myself.

Characteristics of the sample. The 659 New Haven respondents are in no sense a random sample of New Haven school children and, therefore, I have not used statistical inference except as a rule of thumb to identify stable class and sex differences for discussion in Chapters 5 and 6. The "sample" consists of the fourth through eighth grade populations of one private and three public elementary schools. School A is in an extremely depressed, lower-working-class, slum neighborhood in which, where families are not broken, the breadwinner is an unskilled laborer. School B is in an upper-working-class neighborhood. Skilled and semiskilled workers predominate, but there are some unskilled workers and a smattering of white-collar families at the periphery of the district. (The latter are represented only in the seventh and eighth grade groups of School B; these grades draw from a more extended district than grades four through six.) School C serves mainly white-collar families, in business, professional, and lower clerical occupations, but about a third of the school district overlaps a working-class neighborhood. School D is a private grammar school. Tuition is quite high and the children are from prosperous business and professional families. A good number of children of Yale faculty attend School D.

Because of the nonrandom character of the sample, which does not represent socioeconomic status (SES) groups in proportion to their strength in the population, and because SES influences responses, findings were analyzed by a dichotomous socioeconomic status classification, distinguishing roughly between children of white- and blue-collar occupational backgrounds. (The control for SES also was necessary because the proportion of upper and lower SES children varies by school year level—largely because the extended district of the seventh and eighth grades of School B increases the proportion of lower SES children in the older groups.) Reporting by homogeneous SES groups helps compensate for these sampling deficiencies and therefore adds to the generalizability of the New Haven findings, since it becomes possible to make comparisons with similar SES groups in different communities. In general, the overall relationships found in this study were evident in both upper and lower SES groups—the latter (see Chapter 5) are simply less politically informed and involved than the former at every age level. Where SES differences are not relevant to a set of findings, as in Chapters 3 and 6, I have not reported them.

School records and children's reports proved to be unreliable indicators of parental occupation. Therefore it was necessary to rely upon neighborhood as an indicator of SES, coding the child's home address on the basis of a detailed classification of New Haven neighborhoods into six socioeconomic groupings. The classification, which had been made some seven years earlier by a team of Yale sociologists, was based upon value of one-family homes and average monthly rent in each city block and on a five per cent sample of New Haven households. A discussion of classification and, more generally, of New Haven social structure is available in August B. Hollingshead and Fredrick C. Redlich, *Social Class and Mental Illness* (New York, Wiley, 1958). In controlling for SES, I combined children from areas I through III in a group designated upper SES (N=226) and children in areas IV through VI in another group designated lower SES (N=433). As it happened, somewhat more than 85 per cent of the New Haven respondents were in neighborhoods classified as I and II or V and VI which, at the time of the classification, were almost exclusively homogeneous in terms of whether their residents were in blue- or white-collar occupations. This presumably increased the likelihood that children, characterized as upper or lower SES, were indeed from homogeneous and mutually exclusive status groups.

The New Haven findings were analyzed by school classrooms as well as by SES, since the climates of individual schools and classrooms in some cases may account for seeming SES differences (or may suppress SES differences). Because of the class composition of the four schools, at each school year level there were at least two classrooms which contained virtually only lower SES children (classrooms from Schools A and B), one classroom which was exclusively upper SES

TABLE B.1. Composition of New Haven Political Socialization Sample by Neighborhood Classification, School Year, and School

School Year	I*	II	III	IV	V	VI	Total Cases	I*	II	III	IV	V	VI	Total Cases
	School A							School B						
4					4%	96%	(25)					100%		(21)
5					9	91	(22)					100		(32)
6					12	88	(25)					100		(29)
7					12	88	(26)				16%	76	8%	(62)
8					8	92	(39)				21	73	5	(94)
Total					9	91	(137)				13	83	4	(238)
	School C							School D						
4	20%	41%	2%	34%	2%		(44)	90%	5%	5%				(21)
5	37	44	0	16	2		(43)	95	5	0				(21)
6	23	36	3	38	0		(25)	100	0	0				(22)
7	23	42	0	35	0		(26)	95	5	0				(21)
8	20	43	3	30	3		(30)	100	0	0				(17)
Total	25	41	2	30	2		(168)	96	3	1				(102)

*Roman numerals indicate neighborhood classifications. Neighborhoods I-III are grouped in the analysis and referred to as upper SES. Neighborhoods IV-VI are grouped and referred to as lower SES. At the time of the classification, the proportion of college educated in each of the six neighborhoods was: I (65 per cent); II (50 per cent); III (24 per cent); IV (13 per cent); V (9 per cent); VI (5 per cent).

(from School D), and one which was preponderantly (62–82 per cent) upper SES (School C). In the few instances where classroom seemed to have an effect, I have reported on classroom influences. SES differences, such as those showing lower-status children to be less issue oriented, are evidently not merely differences in classroom climate, since we find that the classrooms in both School A and School B consistently differ from those in Schools C and D. As noted in Chapter 5, information about the formal aspects of government does seem to vary by classroom. Classrooms in Schools A and B, which were exposed to intensive social studies teaching, score higher than classrooms at the same school year levels in Schools C and D. For a similar effect, see p. 98.

TABLE B.2. Ethnic Composition of the New Haven Political Socialization Study Sample, by School*

	School A	School B	School C	School D
Major Groups				
English	1%	3%	15%	34%
Irish	4	4	14	3
Italian	40	50	18	1
Jewish	1	6	7	5
Negro	15	5	0	0
Other Groups				
East European	5	8	4	1
Portuguese	6	2	0	0
Puerto Rican	5	0	0	0
Mixed	6	8	6	14
Other	4	4	8	8
Don't Know and No Answer	14	10	29	34
Total cases	(137)	(238)	(182)	(102)

*Ethnic classification was based upon the item at the head of Part I of the questionnaire on place of residence of relatives before coming to the United States. "Don't know" responses ordinarily indicate native stock (usually upper SES) children. It was not possible to use items on race or religion. Negroes were identified by the teachers. Jews were identified by last name and by references to attending Hebrew school in item 18, Part I. The proportion of Jewish children probably is somewhat underestimated.

Further indications of the social composition of the New Haven sample are given in Table B.1, which reports the proportion of children in each of the four schools in the six neighborhood classifications, and Table B.2, which reports the ethnic composition of the four schools.

A more extensive discussion of procedure in the New Haven study may be found in Fred I. Greenstein, "Children's Political Perspectives: A Study of the Development of Political Awareness and Preferences among Pre-Adolescents," unpublished doctoral dissertation, Yale University Library, 1959.

Appendix C

Studies of Children's Exemplars

The following remarks provide additional information about the studies of children's exemplars summarized in Table 7.1 (p. 138) and my reanalysis of these studies. Each is listed here simply by author's name and estimated date of field work; full citations appear in Chapter 7, note 2. There are additional methodological remarks in the footnote to Table 7.1.

Chambers – 1902: The author presents an inventory only of names referred to by more than .4 per cent of the respondents. However, the remainder of his discussion deals extensively (by occupation) with the total array of responses, making it possible to estimate his precise findings closely. My estimate of the percentage of references to "serious" entertainers in his study may be slightly more than three percentage points too low; the actual per cent of "non-serious" entertainers may be a fraction of a per cent lower or higher than my estimate. The estimate of "other" politicians may be a fraction of a per cent high. It was impossible to estimate the possible upper limit of the "other national heroes" category precisely. A small proportion of the responses now grouped under "miscellaneous figures from the wider environment" may have fallen in this category. This deficiency does not affect the conclusion drawn from the table that choice of national heroes as exemplars has declined over the years. The percentage of immediate environment exemplars was estimated by averaging percentages reported for each age group and adjusting for the smaller number of cases in extreme age groups on the basis of information given by Chambers in the text. Much of Chambers' data is presented by sex. Since the sexes are evenly divided in the population he studies, it was possible to combine these percentages. Respondents constituted the entire elementary school population of New

Castle, which the author describes as "a busy industrial city" with a "very heterogeneous population. Among the 40,000 inhabitants are large proportions of English, Welsh, Irish, Scotch, Germans, Italians, Negroes, Swedes. . . . All grades of society, all occupations, all degrees of wealth and intelligence, all kinds of religion are represented."

Hill – 1910: In this and the 1928 Southern study, references to heroes of the Confederacy are common. These have been classified as "other national heroes." The author presents an inventory of all references to public figures with the exception of 23 responses which are placed in a miscellaneous category. His remarks make it clear that a few of the latter exemplars were popular entertainers. Therefore, although only one popular entertainer is mentioned in the inventory, I have estimated the actual number of references to this category at five (.3 per cent). In addition, I was unable to identify the names of exemplars referred to by eight children and have assigned these to the "miscellaneous wider environment" category. Hill reports that his respondents are white children in two public schools. "One school is situated in a somewhat new and popular residential section; the other in an old but, perhaps on the whole, less prosperous locality."

Hill – 1928: The inclusion of 17- to 20-year-old respondents in this study reduces its comparability. However, the distortion is mitigated by the fact that there were few cases in this age group—only five per cent of the respondents were over 16 years of age. In addition, Hill presents some categories of his findings by age, making possible rough estimates of the skew introduced by having adolescents in the sample. He lists the names of all exemplars mentioned more than ten times and the number of references to each. He then presents another listing of the names of all other exemplars, indicating the total number of references to individuals included in this listing. I have assigned the mean value to each such name. Names so listed were referred to by about ten per cent of the respondents. I was unable to identify the names of exemplars mentioned by 1.3 per cent of the respondents. Hill's data, which are presented by sex, are here combined. He comments that his respondents are "white children selected from the enrollment of the public schools of the three largest cities of Alabama. . . . The populations involved comprise an overwhelmingly large proportion of the native-born, of Scotch, Irish, and English descent."

Stoughton and Ray – 1944: This study was of 344 second, fourth, and sixth grade children. I have retabulated the findings to include only the latter two grades, since this brings the mean age of respondents closer to that of the other studies. Retabulation is possible because the authors present a detailed breakdown of findings by school year in categories which are quite similar to those used here. In addition, they discuss extensively the kinds of exemplars mentioned by children in their study and they present an inventory of exemplars, tabulating by school year all names referred to by two or more children and listing slightly more than half of the remaining names mentioned. By comparing the authors' categorized findings and the material in their inventories, the possible estimation errors in my retabulation may be determined precisely: Thus in Table 7.1, it is estimated that 8.1 per cent of the children referred to "non-serious" entertainers. This percentage could have been as high as 11.6, however. Similarly, the percentage of references to "other" politicians is estimated at .4, but if all of the exemplars Stoughton and Ray placed in their "news and contemporary affairs" category without also listing them in the inventory had been politicians, the percentage would have been 3.5. In each of these cases, using the lowest possible estimate is conservative with respect to the argument in the text. By the same logic, the estimate of "other" national heroes in Table 7.1 is as high as could have been possible (4.6 per cent). In fact, no more than 1.5 per cent of the sample may have referred to this category. It is also conceivable (although the authors' discussion suggests it is quite unlikely) that some of the unlisted exemplars may have been business figures (3.1 per cent at the most) and some may have been "serious" entertainers (3.4 per cent at the most). Neither of these outcomes would affect the conclusions of this paper. Stoughton and Ray comment that the schools from which their population was drawn "are situated in cosmopolitan neighborhoods where the families lived in average economic circumstances. A number of nationalities were represented."

In this study the proportion of references to "miscellaneous wider environment figures" (33.4 per cent) and "immediate environment figures" (44.4 per cent) is a good bit higher than in the other studies; hence relatively few cases fall into the categories of exemplar analyzed in the present paper. A number of factors seem to contribute to the size of these two "irrelevant" categories. The greater reference to immediate environment figures seems to be a result of the fact that the mean age of the respondents is somewhat lower than in other studies —references to the wider environment tend to increase with age in these studies. The immediate environment response in this study is only about five per cent higher than it is for comparable age groups in Hill's 1928 study. The size of the miscellaneous category is in part inflated by the gaps referred to above in the authors' inventory of exemplars. A fourth of the cases in this category represent exemplars whose names were not listed and who might conceivably have been classifiable in other categories. Another 15 per cent of the miscellaneous exemplars in this wartime study are military figures, a category which is represented with much less frequency in the other studies. Finally, about seven per cent of the references are to fictional characters in the mass media (Dick Tracy, Superman, etc.), a class of response which is unrepresented in the other studies. These references might possibly have been included among the "non-serious" entertainers, which would have strengthened the already clearly evident trend over the years in this category.

Greenstein – 1958: Findings were retabulated from the original questionnaires for the present analysis.

Index